Dealing with
Difficult
Men

Dealing
with
► DIFFICULT MEN ◄

JUDITH SEGAL, Ph.D.

Lowell House
Los Angeles

Contemporary Books
Chicago

Library of Congress Cataloging-in-Publication Data

Segal, Judith, Ph.D.
    Dealing with difficult men / Judith Segal.
        p. cm.
    ISBN 1-56565-079-4
    1. Men. 2. Men—Psychology. 3. Interpersonal relations. I. Title.
    HQ1090.S42 1993
    305.31—dc20   93-11784
                                                                CIP

Requests for such permissions should be addressed to:

Lowell House
2029 Century Park East, Suite 3290
Los Angeles, CA 90067

Publisher: Jack Artenstein
Vice-President/Editor-in-Chief: Janice Gallagher
Director of Publishing Services: Mary D. Aarons
Text Design: Susan H. Hartman

Manufactured in the United States of America
10 9 8 7 6 5 4 3 2 1

▶ CONTENTS ◀

▶ AUTHOR'S NOTE ◀

This book is geared toward helping you with difficult men who are "normal neurotics," not pathological deviants. If the difficult man you are dealing with is physically, verbally, or emotionally abusive, you need to get professional help immediately. If he is threatening you in any way, you must take the necessary steps to protect yourself. There are many excellent resources available. You don't have to go it alone. Please, do it now.

► ACKNOWLEDGMENTS ◄

I would like to express my appreciation to the many women who have been so generous with their time, feedback, information, and support: Karen Arden, Sunny Bernstein, Marilyn Curland, Judith B. Davis, Teri Donnelly, Mimi Grabis, Diane Gray, B.J. Hateley, Jeanne Hartley, Dianna L. Ho, Patricia Howard, Jerilyn Katzer, Melanie King, Ellen Lachtman, Georgeta Marghidan, Deborah Pinksy, Susan Salenger, Melissa Smith, Lois Snepinger, Donna Stellini, and Dianne Wehner.

I would also like to thank the many others who, because of their desire to keep their personal and professional relationships intact, have chosen to remain anonymous. I thank these women for their willingness to share so much of themselves, especially when it meant remembering some very painful experiences.

I am grateful to my editor, Janice Gallagher, who, throughout the process of writing this book, has been an invaluable coach; my literary agent, Alyss Barlow Dorese, for her guidance and direction; Joyce Mills, who typed the manuscript; Lynne T. Jewell and Fran Krimston for setting the wheels in motion; and Julie Johnson (JJ) who was always there to keep me focused, healthy and laughing.

And last and most significant, I want to thank my husband, Wayne S. Litwin, whose humor, advice (which I didn't always take), thought-provoking questions, and patience were an important reminder to me that not all men are difficult (all of the time).

The
Dealing-With-Difficult-Men
Challenge

As far as men go, the world is full of frogs and princes and many of us have had to deal with much more croaking than we care to remember. What's the ratio of frogs to princes in your life?

As I travel across the United States and Canada, giving seminars and coaching men and women on all aspects of human relations, management, and organization development, I hear the same stories over and over again from women. They complain about obnoxious, inappropriate, and seemingly unconscious men. They all say the same thing: men are difficult, and there is nothing they can do about it. Since I know this isn't true—that there is something they can do about it—I take delight in teaching them how to turn things around so that they no longer have to feel like lily pads, landing strips for those frustrating frogs.

It seems as though I have been in training to write this book for a long, long time. Negotiating to get spending money from my father while I was growing up was the beginning of my own course in the politics of getting what I wanted from a man who was generous with love and difficult (read: careful) with money. I used to yell "moth alert" every time he opened his wallet, because I realized that if I could make him laugh, I had a better chance of softening him up.

As a little girl, I also learned that I could get what I wanted by flirting, whining, or crying, a repertoire that definitely turned out to be limiting in later life. As a teenager, I was self-conscious and insecure. My life was geared toward making boys like me, having a date with one on Saturday night, and not letting any of them know how smart I really was.

It was not surprising that, at age 19, I married a man just because he asked me, and a few years later, divorce papers in hand, I was still a marshmallow. When a man I was dating would say, "You're not hungry, are you?" and I could hardly hear him over the rumbling in my stomach, I invariably answered, "No, not in the least. Are you?" When the mechanic who worked on my car estimated that my bill would be $200 and later called to say that the bill would be $2,000, I actually thanked him in advance for doing the job.

Many years have passed. Not only have I changed, but the men I choose to have around me today and the behavior I am willing to accept have also changed. The best example is my husband, Wayne. Wayne is self-confident and funny, and provides me with regular target-practice opportunities. What makes him a noble and worthy opponent is that he is always willing to discuss any issue that is important to me or to him.

But enough about me; let's talk about you. You opened this book because the title hit home for you. You thought of the difficult men in your life, past and present, and were curious about your options.

Let me tell you, up front, that reading this book will help you take that giant step toward developing the skills you'll need in order to do what must be done: not to hate men—on the contrary, to learn how to deal with the difficult ones effectively and, in so doing, allow yourself to appreciate and really enjoy the "good" ones.

Dealing with stressed, confused, manipulative, and, in some cases, seemingly unconscious men takes skill, knowledge, experience, and resilience. What you say and the way you say it to them is important. The way you feel about yourself before, during, and after is crucial. Ask yourself whether you feel powerful or powerless in your relationships with difficult men. Are you where you want to be or still working on getting there?

Face it, you can't get men to stop using difficult behavior without learning how to position yourself so that you're strong but not at their expense, assertive without being overmanipulative or subversive, and direct without being overbearing. Dumping on difficult men is not the answer. Changing the rules so that they can't dump on you is.

You can learn to stay in control of yourself, to package yourself to be "tamper-proof." You can learn to take care of yourself and take care of business at the same time. You can learn to stand your ground and feel confident enough to talk to any difficult man at any time about anything you choose.

What makes the men in your life difficult? I have found that difficult men seem to have three characteristics in common. First, they are in some way what I call communicatively challenged. Whether they are hiding their opinions or feelings or pushing them on you with great intensity, their communication is not clear, open, or direct, and it is certainly not honest. Second, these difficult men, whether they are totally withholding of their feelings, totally unaware that they even have feelings, or out of control and blasting their feelings, are emotional Neanderthals. If they have any emotions at all, they hide them well, are ruled by them, or are totally out of touch with them. And last but not least is the issue of these difficult men and control. Whether they control you with their passive behavior or their bluntly aggressive acting out, they all show signs of being control freaks.

Regardless of the reasons, what matters is that you learn to deal with them. It's not practical to waste time wondering or worrying when you could be on your way to changing things and taking back your power. It's time you gained the confidence and communication skills that will put you in control of yourself and your situation. It's time you adjusted your thinking so that you stop acting and feeling like a victim. It's time you armed yourself with the body language and the words that will get you through any difficult-man situation. So roll up your sleeves, turn to chapter 1, and dig in!

1

Men Are Difficult
and
We Allow It

Recently, waiting for a flight back to Los Angeles, I had an opportunity to indulge in one of my favorite pastimes: eavesdropping. An obviously affluent, middle-aged woman and her husband were sitting right next to me, reading—he, the *Wall Street Journal*, and she, *Better Homes & Gardens*. As I was discreetly checking them out, she stood up, turned to him, casually put her hand out, and said, "Give me a few dollars, please." He looked up at her, slowly and deliberately put down his paper, and said, "Just exactly what do you need it for?"

Here was a grown woman being grilled by her husband. Now I was really hooked. I continued my eavesdropping with even more enthusiasm and heard her reply, "I just want to get another magazine" to which he said firmly, in an impatient, scolding tone, "You don't need another one. Just sit down and wait for our flight to board." And she did. She sat down, picked up her old magazine and flipped through the pages. This woman allowed the man she was with to be difficult, and I don't know whether she even thought much about it.

I myself grew up thinking that this type of conversation and power relationship was normal between men and women. It wasn't so much that my parents related this way, because they didn't; but it was all around me: on television; in newspapers, magazines, and novels. It was everywhere.

I keep wanting to think that times have changed, and for some people they might have. We now live in a time when men and women are faced with dealing with each other in new and different ways. There are more two-career couples. Women are more involved in all aspects of our society. The demands made on both sexes have changed from what we expected growing up or even what we may have become accustomed to. It's a new day. Or is it?

Today, the relationships that we, as women, have with men can be wonderful or frustrating, funny or depressing. Most of the time, though, relationships with men are complicated, mixing up power, sex, and status. That's why I want to say this now and get it out of the way: As you read this book, remember that while not all men are difficult, a lot of them really are. I don't think that I know one woman who has not had to deal with a difficult man at some point in her life. In fact, some days, for a lot of the women I encounter, it almost seems as though they function as magnets for difficult men. Have you noticed this, and have you also noticed that some men are difficult to some women and not to others? We have to ask ourselves how this happens, and when we do that, we, as women, have to take some responsibility for men continuing to be as difficult as they are.

Can we agree that although not all men are difficult, enough of them are to warrant some serious attention? Good. Let's continue then.

● THE DEALING-WITH-DIFFICULT-MEN PLAN

This book will equip you with the tools you need to make the changes you want with the difficult men in your life.

Here is our game plan. In order to change the way difficult men treat us, we first have to understand and acknowledge exactly what our situation is, how it got to be this way, and what we, as women, do to perpetuate it. We do have some responsibility, and we have to own up to it if we want to make things better. So, the rest of chapter 1 will talk about all these things, including how to recognize a severe case of Testosterone Deference Syndrome. You'll also get a chance to understand the myth of testicular power and how it holds us back. Once we understand where we are and how we got here, we will take the next step of assessing the difficult men we attract in our lives. Some women keep on attracting different types of difficult men, and others seem to find the same type over and over again. The "Are You a Difficult-Man

Magnet?" Quiz at the end of this chapter will quickly allow you to identify whom you're attracting and whether or not your condition is "localized."

In chapter 2, we'll look for some specific reasons why you are attracting those men. We'll begin to examine the different types of difficult men in all areas of our lives, from the Blamer and the Destroyer to the Wimp and Mama's Precious, with many others in between. We'll look at who they are, what makes them tick, and what makes them keep on ticking. We'll go right to the heart of the issue, looking at specific words and behaviors to use with the different types of difficult men who are making unwelcome appearances in your life. If you want a buffet of techniques to choose from, this is where you can get it, from soup to nuts. After you've read this chapter, these guys won't stand a chance; they'll be totally exposed for who and what they are.

Chapter 3, your attitude-adjustment chapter, will take you through all the moves you have to make to take control of yourself and your relationships. It will give you the vision that you need to decide to change the way men treat you and show you how to stop worrying about what they think and start focusing on what you want.

We will begin at the beginning, examining and adjusting your attitude, because if you think like a winner, you'll be a winner. If you expect to be treated well, you'll do whatever you need to do in order to make it happen. Once you've adjusted your attitude, you will be ready to go into training. If we were going on a rock-climbing expedition, we'd have to psych ourselves up, get the right equipment, and learn some basic techniques.

What we are doing here is no different. Once you've got your self-talk sounding better, you've got to work on how you approach and talk to difficult men.

Chapter 4 will arm you to make all the difference that we talk about in chapter 2. Imagine how great it will feel to know all the important skills and how to use them and be ready to appropriately confront any difficult man about anything. Think of the satisfaction you'll get out of having some all-purpose comebacks and the great pride you'll take in breaking your old, damaging habits, even the ones you don't yet know you have. We'll discover when and how to use difficult men as target practice. I can hardly wait!

Then it's on to chapter 5, a step-by-step guide to conflict savvy. We want to make sure that your strategy and timing are properly set and that you are perfectly ready to go from start to finish, with no questions and problems in between. I don't know about you, but I hate to waste time or energy. Once I do something, I want to do it right, get what I want, and then move on and forget about it. At this point it will be important to take time out for a safety or reality check. Again, the idea is to deal with difficult men (a) who are worth it and (b) when you have a chance of being successful. This chapter will help you do the same. That is not to say, however, that these men will like the way you are dealing with them, which is why we move on to chapter 6.

Chapter 6 is about backlash and coping with negative reactions. This will be very important, so don't stop before you get there. This is where you will understand more about change and how different people, especially difficult-men people, react to it so negatively at times. We'll talk about the difficult men who "liked you better when..." and give you some directions on how to formulate plans for when some difficult men launch a counterattack or instigate countermaneuvers.

Finally, and deservedly so, we arrive at chapter 7, which will describe how to deal with success and enjoy new types of relationships with men who are no longer difficult (with you). We'll cement your new skills and keep you from backsliding.

Does all this sound like a lot of ground to cover? It is a lot, but it is also going to be a great adventure. *Dealing with Difficult Men* is designed specifically to help you achieve whatever you want. The possibilities are endless, and so are the opportunities.

IT'S UP TO US

Keep this in mind. The key to dealing with difficult men is to look at each difficult man as a potential growth experience, another experiment in your trial-and-error method of taking control of yourself, your relationships, and your life. Some men don't mean to be difficult, and some men are amazed when it is suggested to them that they are being difficult. They look at you with amazement as if to say, "*Moi?* Surely, you jest." Well, guess what, buddy. We jest not.

Ask any woman what makes men difficult and you'll get similar answers:

> *"They feel threatened by any type of assertiveness or aggression."*

> *"They equate being difficult with being a 'man' or manly. They believe they're supposed to be this way."*

> *"They're insecure about everything — from their performance in the bedroom to their performance in the boardroom."*

So we understand what they're doing; we know how it can make us feel; and still, *we put up with it!* Many women with whom I've spoken say the same thing about the dilemma:

> *"Most of the time, when a guy is being difficult, the* woman allows it. *She accepts it and reinforces it. She doesn't say, 'Knock it off!'"*

> *"As women, what we do to promote difficult behavior is to work more on an emotional level. We personalize things; we sound gushy; we say things like "I feel" instead of "I want."*

When male coworkers are creating problems, for example, many women turn them into emotional issues and unknowingly make the situation worse by discounting themselves. This is how they operate in their personal lives as well. As a result, husbands discount wives who resort to crying, complaining, or "worse," wanting to talk about hurt feelings.

Let's take a moment to examine what we know about difficult men and how we, as women, deal with their behavior. Men don't change because we want them to, and they don't even change because we think they should. They change because they decide that it is appropriate, that there is something in it for them, or that their old behavior no longer works. An old saying goes, "You can't teach a pig to sing; you waste your time and annoy the pig." In order to get men to sing, we have to make them want to sing; and so far we haven't been doing this at all.

Instead, as women, we tend to help men cement their old, dysfunctional ways of acting. We overlook the miserable things they do, and we have for years. We say, "Boys will be boys," instead of, "This man is acting like a jerk." We say, "He doesn't mean any harm," instead of, "I want him to care."

Yes, we make it easier for men to be difficult. We roll out the red carpet, put a light in the window, glue a dart board to our forehead, and hand them the darts.

Well, enough is enough. It is not up to men to decide to change when they feel like it. A lot of men will never feel like it, and why should they? Life is good. Women defer. Things are just dandy for them, thank you very much.

Let's make a deal with ourselves and each other. This process of dealing with difficult men is not about being more of a man than they are, outsmarting them at their own game, or acting like Superbitch, if you will pardon my language. The changes that need to happen are in us. We put up the barriers, and we can take them down. When you see a difficult man approaching, roll up the red carpet and take out the microscope instead. Let's put the difficult man on a slide and take a good look at him to understand what we're dealing with, then put ourselves on the same slide and really examine our part and work on ourselves. In other words, we acknowledge his behavior but focus on ours.

● GROWING UP DEFERENTIAL

As girls, most of us grow up deferring to boys. We value boys more than other girls and begin setting them upon their thrones at a very early age. I can remember feeling like a failure as a teenager when I didn't have a date on Saturday night. As a consolation, I would make plans with girlfriends, but if a boy would happen to call, even at seven o'clock that night, it was "Good-bye, girl-friends." Any old date in a storm.

In school, teachers always looked to boys for the right answers. Boys were expected to take more risks, be more independent, look after themselves, and look after girls. They grew up believing that they were hot stuff, and we grew up believing it, too.

After I completed my master's degree, I became interested in what made women act the way they did, which led me to study human sexuality. I took extensive training, and before beginning my doctorate in human development, I progressed to graduate instructor. For years, when I taught graduate courses in human sexuality to therapists, clergy, nurses, police, and other groups, I asked the women in my classes to list the messages that they got about how girls and women are and how boys and men should be and asked the men to do the same thing in reverse: to write down how men and boys are and how girls and women should be.

Regardless of the classes, the lists were almost always identical. I have given you what most of them repeated, time after time.

This is what the women said:

Girls and women are:	Boys and men should be:
Money spenders, not moneymakers	Superior to women
	Stronger
Here to make people happy	Smarter
Supposed to smile	Better drivers
	Coordinated
Emotional	Confident
Sexual—but not too sexual	Breadwinners
Supposed to say "thank you"	Financially secure
	Taller
Not supposed to talk back	Sexually dominant

(continued)

Girls and women are:	Boys and men should be:
Supposed to be prudish until they get married and then only a little bit prudish	Always on top
	Presidents
	Studs
Not supposed to get angry	Politically aggressive
Not supposed to let boys know that they're smart	Doctors
Not supposed to ask too many questions	Lawyers
	Demanding
Bad drivers	Masculine
Soft	Cool
Always dieting	Sophisticated
Naive	Horny
Self-conscious	With-it
Fickle	Sly
Temperamental	Clever
Ignorant	Hairy
Usable	
Jealous	
Mothers	
Inexperienced	
Hard to understand	

This is what the men said:

Boys and men are:	Girls and women should be:
Rough	Shorter than boys
Tough	Virgins
Strong	Respectable
Good lovers	Soft-spoken
Insensitive	Naive
Selfish	Graceful
Egotistical	Feminine
Unemotional	Slim
Competitive	Big-busted
Possessive	A saint in the home and a whore in bed
Athletic	
Mechanically inclined	Maternal
	Faithful
Domineering	Poised
Bread-winners	Mothers
Unfaithful	Less trustworthy
Vain	Subservient
Uncaring	Ladies
	Clean
	Good cooks
	Patient
	Creative

Isn't it amazing—and horrifying? So much damage has been done on both sides. Just comparing the two lists gives us a very clear picture of how the way we were raised has worked against us. It has set us back and left us unprepared for dealing with difficult men and sometimes for life in general. Many women allow men to be difficult because they bought the myth and don't think they have a right to anything different.

Most women who have gone through my seminars, either sexuality or management, have one thing in common: for some portion of their lives, beginning in childhood, they believed that it was their job to make men happy, to gain approval from men, and to defer to men. They all believed that it was inappropriate to outwardly demand anything from men and that they ought to feel grateful to have a man, any man. When we believe these things, we automatically give difficult men permission to be so, and we strip ourselves of the ability to assert our wants and our needs.

A lot of women have never given themselves permission to be dissatisfied with the men in their lives, at work or at home. They've felt dissatisfaction, not to mention alienation and resentment, but they haven't believed that they deserved any better.

Keep in mind that we're talking about ideas and beliefs that have been chiseled into our minds, our bodies, and our beings from day one. Girls were raised not to correct boys, and boys were raised to correct and, if need be, criticize girls. Girls were raised to say no but somehow imply yes; boys were raised to say yes and mean it or no and mean it. As women, most of us were raised to make men feel needed, and we were raised to be helpless. We were raised to doubt ourselves, and it shows! Difficult men know it, and they use it against us.

Think about yourself. Do you believe that you have to be sure not to ask questions, either because they'll make you look too smart or too stupid? I cannot tell you how many times women in my seminars have began their questions by saying, "This is probably a stupid question, but..."

Ask yourself, do I believe that it's okay to say no, or that saying no will make me seem rude and inconsiderate? Do I believe that if people around me are miserable, I should have done, or am supposed to do, something to make them feel better? Can I relate to the idea that I should not tell the truth if it means that I might hurt someone's feelings? If your answer to these questions is yes, then the way you were raised is keeping you subservient to difficult men.

● THE TESTOSTERONE DEFERENCE SYNDROME

When Clarissa was married to her ex-husband, she deferred a lot and abdicated responsibility, then blamed him for her not getting what she wanted. She helped him to be more difficult. She colluded—unknowingly and unintentionally. Following is an example of what she used to do.

Clarissa and her husband, along with her friend and

her friend's husband were going skiing. She woke up early that morning, put on her ski pants, and promptly broke the zipper. "No big deal," she said to her husband, while he watched her throw the offending clothing on the bed. "I'll wear jeans. It's not that cold and not that slushy. I'll be fine." "No way," he said. "You're not going. You cannot ski in jeans. I won't allow it." So she actually stayed home, alone. And it wasn't even his behind that ran the risk of freezing. She was in her early twenties, he was treating her like a child, and *she allowed it!* Can you imagine? If there is such a thing as retroactive embarrassment, she actually experienced it, blushing, twenty years later, while recounting the story to me.

At the time, though, she laughed when she told her woman friend that she would be going without her. She made a joke about her husband taking "such good care" of her (which he really believed he was doing). But inside she felt small, powerless, embarrassed, and humiliated. It took a long time for her to realize that it didn't have to be this way, that her feelings were valid, and that she could make decisions for herself instead of deferring to someone else.

After she had been divorced for a year from her husband, he invited her to dinner. As they sat in the restaurant they made small talk, and he told her about his latest acquisitions. When he finished, she began telling him about how excited she was about going back to school. At that point, he stopped chewing his steak and looked at her quizzically. "Why are you doing all this?" he asked her with true amazement in his voice. "How will getting all this education make you a better wife and mother?"

Even though the sentence was phrased like a question, she realized that it really was a statement.

She opened her mouth to begin to dispute his remark and then she said to herself, "Why bother?" This was his way of thinking and his way of communicating, and, thank goodness, she remembered that they were divorced.

But before we rush on, I think this is worth another minute, since it brings up some basic rules that I will tell you about later in the book. Clarissa had to ask herself, when this happened, did she have a chance of changing his mind? She answered, "No way." Did he want to change his mind? Not on your life. Had he found a woman who saw things his way, or at least was prepared to accept them? Yes, indeed. Therefore, her chances of making a difference weren't even slim. They were nonexistent.

Here is a preview of one of my tips to you. Don't play if:

a. You can't win

b. You don't care

c. You're not ready

This time, Clarissa chose "b." True, "a" was also applicable. But "b" was where her heart was, or wasn't.

Think about all the different ways that women defer to men. Barbara described one "deference" work relationship she had with a difficult professional associate:

> "In front of the client, my associate was question-
> ing me about things that he should have

known. Why was he doing it? To test me? Well, that was partially right. He was also doing it to establish control and superiority. And the client responded just as he wanted her to. She addressed all subsequent questions and comments to him and totally ignored me.

Glenda remembers how a certain man used all his resources for his own unique type of power-playing, until she realized that she didn't have to defer. She could head him off in her own unique way.

"I dated a very handsome man who used to play a game and stare at me piercingly with his absolutely gorgeous eyes. I could just tell that he knew how mesmerizing and unnerving they were. One day, over dinner, I looked at him and said, 'You know you have the most gorgeous eyes, and I can't help but think that it's a sin that those eyelashes are on you, instead of on me.' After that, the relationship changed. He stopped playing the game, and I felt totally comfortable. But I noticed that when we were with other women, he would pull the same stuff. The women would blush, look down, and defer to him."

Many women are intimidated by extremely attractive or nonresponsive men. They play up to the men, reinforcing their behavior.

Let's take a closer look at Testosterone Deference

Syndrome so that you can discover whether or not you suffer from it. Don't worry if you do, since it is curable. Most women have at least a mild case of it. It's difficult not to if you were raised in North America. June and Ward Cleaver in *Leave It to Beaver* modeled it, and Jim and Margaret Anderson in *Father Knows Best* made it an art form. Ozzie and Harriet brought it to new heights, and let's not even bring up *The Brady Bunch*.

The problem is that TDS can be so very subtle that even I have to catch myself when I'm in conversation with a group of men and women, because it is often easier to talk and listen to men and to ignore other women. Many women have a different way of presenting their ideas. They usually don't present them as law, and they often don't sound as authoritative as men do. As a result, we assume that men have the power. It is amazing how often women look through other women to get to the men. For example, when I call a restaurant to make a reservation, the conversation goes like this, whether the person taking the reservation is male or female:

> *"I'd like a reservation for two at 7:30 tonight."*
> *"Of course, What is the name?"*
> *"Dr. Segal."*
> *"Thank you. That's tonight, for two, at 7:30. Please tell Dr. Segal that his table will be ready."*

I rest my case.

Do a quick Testosterone Deference Syndrome spot check. Do you:

- Pay more attention to what a man says than you do to what a woman says?

- Ask "who" when in general conversation someone uses "she" instead of "he"?

- Look more at men than at women when you are talking to both at the same time?

- Worry about what men will think of you?

- Take more time and care when you dress to see a man than you do to see a woman?

- Ask men for advice more than you ask women?

- Give in more easily with a man?

- Believe that you always have to try to please a man?

- Put aside what you think and accept what he thinks?

- Shrug your shoulders when you don't want to answer a question?

- Raise the tone of your voice or blush when confronted by a man?

If your answer is yes to at least three of these, you've been afflicted, and the offending microbe is the Myth of Testicular Power.

● THE MYTH OF TESTICULAR POWER

It usually isn't terminal and it doesn't mean you're stupid, but it can inflict a lot of pain and anguish, and millions of women believe it. For some reason, we women grow up thinking that a penis, testicles, and a scrotum add up to more than a vulva, a clitoris, and a vagina. I don't get it. We ignore the rest of the body, we discount the mind, and we defer to the most vulnerable and what some might call the most ridiculous part of the male person.

Stop and think about it. What is the big deal? Can it lift heavy objects? I think not. Can it sniff out a shoe sale? Not to my knowledge. Can it get you bumped up to first class when you're traveling on a "cheapie" ticket? Uh-uh. Why do we make such a fuss about it?

And to think that all this starts when we are really young. I remember a boy laughing at me because I had to sit down to pee, as if spending an extra few minutes on my feet would be such a gift. I don't know about you, but my days are busy, and that is sometimes the only time I do have to sit down.

And will a penis help in the kitchen? Not unless you can use it to punch the buttons on a microwave. And if it can't do that, I'm just not interested. It's no good as a sauce tester, and who wants to use it as a mixing spoon? I ask you: what is the big deal?

Growing up, I was handed a lot of bull about what boys and men were better at, but as an adult woman, I have a choice about what I believe and what I discard. Why do so many women insist upon holding on to the men-are-better-than-women-because-they-have-certain-equipment myth? It holds us back, keeps us down, and, bottom line, it's not true.

● MEN LIKE IT THIS WAY

When men go through a divorce, they usually get a new car, lose a few pounds, and hit the dating scene almost immediately.

Women, on the other hand, look as if they've been run over by a tractor trailer or have gone through the spin cycle of their washing machine on high for about an hour. When men go through a divorce, they are invited to the homes of their "couple" friends much more often than are their estranged wives. This is because many women still believe that men need to be taken care of. So, most men think that they are the way they should be, the way nature intended them to be.

I almost fell off my chair when Barbara told me what had happened to her:

> *"I've been having a relationship with a married man for years now. He comes to town once a year, and we do our thing. He works in my industry. One day, he suggested that we not go to a certain restaurant because there might*

> be some people he knew, and he did not want
> to jeopardize my reputation. 'My reputation?'
> I asked incredulously. 'You're the one who is
> married. What about your reputation?'

> "Oh,' he replied, casually, 'people expect it from a
> man. It's not a big deal the way it is for a
> woman.'"

Let me mention, as an aside, that I know that many people do not see this as laudable behavior on either part. I do see this as an important example, however, of how we function.

If you were the man in this situation, and you had given yourself permission to be unfaithful and proud of it, and you were surrounded by a lot of other men who felt the same way and supported you and your problem, would you want to change? Of course not. *Difficult men like it this way.* They can have their cake and other people's, too. Women buy into it as well, accepting it and making allowances for it.

A woman I know is married to a man with elderly parents and several children from a previous marriage. He is an executive with a large staff and plenty of money and time. So why is it that his wife does all the planning around where and when they will see all the children? Why is it that his wife attends to his parents? How does it happen that he invites people over and expects her to always entertain whom he wants, when he wants, and how he wants? Because *she does it,* and she complains to her friends but says nothing to him.

When I asked her why she doesn't say anything, she sighed "It's not worth getting him upset. That's just he way he is. He'll never change." Darn right, he'll never change! Why should he? I wouldn't, in his position.

We can talk about personal relationships and relationships at work. Difficult men like it the way it is at both places. We hear about women making strides in business, but don't get too excited. Most of them are not striding to the right places. The number of women entering the work force is staggering. The number of women moving into the real executive suites is disappointing. I now believe that every woman who thinks that she won't encounter difficult men is missing the point, because these men are building glass ceilings at alarming rates, making it necessary for women to carry hammers in their purses, just in case. They will need them, and they have to know how and when to use them.

Difficult men flaunt their difficult behavior everywhere. I have seen a lot of men who will sit in a meeting with a supposedly equal female coworker and who, when they want to make a decision without her, will simply retreat to the bathroom for a "pit stop," talk among themselves over the urinals, make the decision, and then go back to the meeting and play it out. It's very effective, and often the woman doesn't even know what's happened. Let's face facts. Many men are not standing at the front doors of their companies applauding women as they enter their formerly male-dominated worlds.

Tell me, if you had a wife at home who took care of your daily needs, even though she, too, had a full-time job, and a woman at the office who took care of you by protecting you, covering for you, and telling you about all the office dirt, and furthermore, if all this nurturing helped you get bigger raises, plum assignments, and more respect, would you want to upset the apple cart? Not likely, and neither do most men. They like it this way for a reason, and the reason is, it works for them.

So far, it hasn't been necessary for difficult men to question their own behavior. But it won't be long now. Let's start by questioning ourselves about our own propensity for attracting one or several varieties of the difficult male species.

● ARE YOU A DIFFICULT-MAN MAGNET?

Think about the men in your life. We can bet that some of them are wonderful, kind, considerate, and interesting—not necessarily easy but not destructive either. Not all of the men in your life are horrible. It's just that there are times when you feel uncomfortable and out of control with some of them.

You may feel used, taken advantage of, talked down to, taken for granted, set up, let down, insulted, foolish, angry, or sad before, during, or after any contact with them. Not to say that these feelings are uncommon—they are not—and not to say that you can't feel these feelings with nondifficult men. You can. What we're talking about here is the relentless, nagging, ungiving, confidence-eroding, and energy-draining stuff; the kind of behavior that makes you feel tired when you've just had a solid eight hours of sleep.

What's that? You're groaning, rolling your eyes, thinking about putting this book down and getting something to eat? Don't give up that easily. Difficult men have to learn that although they can be difficult somewhere else, the rules change when they're with you.

If you've ever wondered if you have "difficult-man radar" because they always seem to end up on your doorstep or in front of your desk at work, you need to find out exactly which specimens you attract. To do this, take the following quiz. Read each of the questions and check off the appropriate characteristics that your difficult men exhibit, and lest you despair, hang on to the fact that you are not in this alone. There are a lot of other wonderful women who are going through this with you.

Sections 1 through 10 represent different composite descriptions of difficult men. Although it's true that all men are different, it is possible to lump some of their behaviors together and come up with some main types, which you'll find in chapter 2. After you complete this quiz, you may find that you have checked off items spread throughout all ten sections or that your selections are clustered together in just one or two. Either way is fine. Your response pattern will indicate whether you're dealing with a "pure" difficult man or a "combo pack."

The "Are You a Difficult-Man Magnet" Quiz

Think about the men you have relationships with at work or at home.

1. Do they:

   ■ Move in and take over? y

   ■ Explode? y

   ■ Push you around, verbally and emotionally? y

   ■ Believe that might makes right, and since they have might of course they're right? y

2. Do they:

   ■ Correct you in front of others? y

   ■ Find fault with you and your ideas? y

   ■ Blame you for everything? √

   ■ Take responsibility for nothing? y

3. Do they:

   ■ See themselves as cool and logical? y

   ■ Resent it when you become emotional? y

   ■ Need to see proof of anything you say? y

   ■ Reject ideas that they don't believe? y

4. Do they:

   ■ Pretend that they care and then make you Y
   feel stupid?

   ■ Keep you guessing and never really open up? Y

   ■ Tell you that you're perfect and then try to Y
   change you?

   ■ Sucker you in and then drop you on your behind? Y

5. Do they:

   ■ Take the best for themselves because they deserve Y
   it and you don't?

   ■ Take charge and tell you what to do? Y

   ■ Distance themselves and refuse to mingle with Y
   "just anyone"?

   ■ Take care of themselves at your expense? Y

6. Do they:

   ■ Try to "pollinate every flower"? Y

   ■ Blow-dry the hair on their chest? Y

   ■ Punt small dogs to make themselves look tough? N

   ■ Believe that the size of their biceps are directly
   proportional to the size of their organs? Y

7. Do they:

   - Puff themselves up? Y

   - Brag as if you should care? Y

   - Tell you they know it all, have seen it all, and have done it all? Y

   - Let you know how little you know? Y

8. Do they:

   - Get cramps when you say the "C" (commitment) y word?

   - Give an immediate disclaimer about not being ready to meet a deadline? Y

   - Always think that you're trying to trap them? Y

   - Convince themselves that you're more serious about the relationship than they are? Y

9. Do they:

   - Always look as if they have been carrying the weight of the world on their shoulders? Y

   - Nice you to death? Y

   - Love being the victim? Y

   - Have one lifelong crisis? Y

10. Do they:

- Worship their mother (or all mothers, for that matter)? *?.*

- Refuse to change their ways? *Y*

- Still live at home, emotionally if not physically? *Y*

- Act more like a little boy than an adult? *Y*

Hang on to your answers. As you proceed to chapter 2, you'll find out what men correspond to these groups, how they operate, and what you can do to change how you deal with them.

The
Lineup

In this part of the process of dealing with difficult men, we will take a very close look at them. A note of caution: you may not want to eat anything just before you do this!

As you read the upcoming descriptions, you will undoubtedly understand why my friend Nora insists that "sperm banks are the only way to go," and you will recognize many types of difficult behavior. You'll also notice that each type is a composite with some overlap from one to another, since these difficult men are a lot like chameleons in that they change to blend into their environments.

Some men are perfectly civil, fun, and easy to be with when alone with women, but put them in a room with other guys and they instantly exhibit a serious behavior metamorphosis. The most polite and genteel guy, when placed in front of a football game with a group of his buddies, will transform himself into a walking, talking, belching machine in about three seconds flat right before your very eyes.

There are also those like the married man Freda worked with, who, although not perfect, seemed quite respectful of women. At least, that's what Freda thought until the morning she heard him talking to one of his buddies about a woman he'd been dating "on the side," and she actually heard him say, "First I'll do her, then I'll tell her." And there are still other types of, shall we say, different attitudes or behavior patterns.

My mother made an interesting observation. While listening to me talk about my research for this book, she was reminded of how many women of her generation married men who seemed capable of making toast or frying an egg but who, after just a few weeks of marriage, developed a serious case of brain drain. They forgot what a frying pan or a toaster was, because they now had a wife to do these things for them. Even though this happened to my mother's contemporaries, it should be noted that these cases are not limited to any one generation, since some of my friends have husbands who lived quite neatly as bachelors and who now forget that dirty clothes go into the hamper or laundry chute, not on the floor next to the bed. This emphasizes that age-old question, Are difficult men born or made? Doesn't matter, as long as you're not the one contributing to their perpetuation.

The purpose of the upcoming lineup is to introduce you to the specific types of men and their behaviors. After the initial description (symptoms), we'll move on to the prescription (treatment). The remaining chapters will give you the appropriate "medicines," tools and techniques to help you fill your prescriptions.

So that it is not overwhelming and to ensure that this examination is manageable, I have classified difficult men by ten types divided into three categories, based on what they most want or need from women. I have set up this classification based on the quiz in chapter 1, so have your results ready.

The first category, the Powermongers, is that of men who want power. Included in this category are the Destroyer (section 1 of The "Are You a Difficult-Man Magnet?" Quiz), the Blamer (section 2), the Logic Pusher (section 3), and the Baiter-and-Switcher (section 4).

The second category, the Admiration Hounds, includes difficult men who want and need admiration from women. You may know the Executive (section 5), the Stud (section 6), or the Self-proclaimed Expert (section 7).

And, as if these aren't enough, stay tuned for our third and final category, comprising difficult men who want and need TLC (tender, loving care) and nurturing: the Nurture Needers. I bet you know the Commitment Phobic (section 8), the Wimp (section 9), and Mama's Precious (section 10). If not, you're lucky, because they are everywhere and multiplying at an alarming rate.

As you read about each of the three categories, instead of searching for the exact description of your difficult man, look for those symptoms that are most representative of the difficult men you deal with.

As I have said, there is no such thing as a "pure" difficult man. By this, I mean that your difficult man may be motivated by power, but a small part of him might also want some nurturing. He might be communicatively challenged when dealing with you but show no signs of this when he is with his buddies. He might be one way with you on Monday and somewhat different on Friday. To deal with such complex behavior, you need an edge, and you're about to get it.

● THE POWERMONGERS

Difficult men motivated by power are not unlike the wolf in the children's story of the three pigs that many of us grew up with. Remember the line "I'll huff and I'll puff and I'll blow your house down?" Well, these guys took it seriously and have made it a way of life. Their basic stance is that women are meant to be conquered and controlled and that they're the ones to do it.

Can you reverse this dysfunctional pattern? No, but you can modify it. Difficult men who push for power need something to push against, and if you stop pushing, you take away the resistance they need to keep from falling on their face.

These are the main types of Powermongers: the Destroyer, the Blamer, the Logic Pusher, and the Baiter-and-Switcher. Let's go through them one at a time.

THE DESTROYER ◀

Description

Destroyers are men who often like to play verbal kickball with you as the ball. These difficult men can be loud and abrasive or quiet and seething. Their intense personalities often explode in anger and inappropriate behavior. At home, they might try to control everything you do. At work, they might yell and embarrass you in front of others. They see only one way—*their* way—and they expect total compliance from you. They use intimidation on a regular basis, sometimes doing it with humor and other times with threats.

The man Pam lived with would build her up with compliments in public, and at home, in private, he would tell her she was a mess. His favorite control technique was the mind game. He'd say things like "You can't make it out there alone. You'll never go anywhere without me. You owe me for all I've done for you."

Not all Destroyers are this intense and destructive. What they are is downright inconvenient to deal with. They have such a short fuse that they are totally unpredictable, or they flex their power by making it uncomfortable for you to refuse to do what they want.

Prescription

Many Destroyers are very enticing, but from the word *go* the Destroyer deliberately sets you up to be at his mercy. He intentionally tries to control you, and you must be prepared either to reduce your resistance if the issue is not important or to be direct and assertive if you are unwilling to comply. These are the techniques you will find outlined in chapter 5, "Conflict Savvy." Also, you can sometimes use humor to defuse the situation, as long as the humor is not self-deprecating or aimed at the Destroyer himself.

The Destroyer uses strength and intensity to feel powerful. So when it makes sense—and *only* then—let him have his way; if you don't have a strong emotional investment (chapter 5), if you can live with it, and if you don't really care, don't go for the win. Avoid the issue. You can give the Destroyer feedback and try to negotiate, but make sure you are emotionally calm and cool enough to attempt this.

Pick low-risk issues to begin with. It is important to define the problem, choose your conflict position by deciding how important it is to you (chapter 5), and adjust your attitude (chapter 3) so that you remember you have a right to work on changing your situation.

Sometimes, leaving a Destroyer is the only way to go; at other times, you can either stand up to him or barter.

Many Destroyers also combine some qualities of the Executive, a member of the Admiration Hounds. Their drive is motivated by their belief that they deserve everything and you deserve nothing. They have no conscience about what they do, and they have no respect or regard for you as a woman, let alone a professional woman.

Dee's boss told her to enter some figures into a report. When he reviewed her work, he thought that what she did was wrong, so he changed the numbers. A week later, her boss's manager called her in and said, "How could you be so stupid? Your numbers are wrong!" Dee went to her boss and said, "Why did you make me take the rap for your mistake?" to which he responded, "Because I'm going up in this company, and you're going nowhere, so it doesn't matter."

What did Dee do? She confronted and gave feedback (chapter 4). She told her boss that she was concerned that he had put a cap on her career development, and she wanted to work with him to develop a career plan. She also went to her boss's boss and told him that there must have been some confusion, because the numbers on the report did not match the numbers on the data sheets she was working from. She also offered him her data sheets. She didn't accuse her boss; she just excused herself.

THE BLAMER ◀

Description

Because of their insecurity, Blamers have a strong emotional investment in saving face. It takes guts and self-esteem to be able to say, "I screwed up," or "Oops, that was no good," and Blamers don't want to take the risk. That's why they find negatives in you. Pointing out what's not okay with you is their way of constantly trying to reaffirm what's okay about themselves. Champion guilt-givers, Blamers raise passive-aggressive behavior to new heights. Since nothing you do is ever right, they are convinced that nothing they ever do is wrong. These guys can be very nasty, and you have to resist the tendency to snap back.

Take Belle's husband, who wanted beef stew for dinner. Belle placed a steaming plate of it on the table in front of him and while she was in the kitchen getting some bread, she heard him scream. When she ran back into the dining room, he was livid, yelling, "Don't you ever, I mean ever, place of plate of hot stew in front of me again!" He had burned his lip.

Here we have a grown man with no apparent disabilities wanting his wife to give him a food-temperature report and to take responsibility for his shoveling it into his mouth without checking it first. A little self-righteous, perhaps? It would serve him right if she gave him a Snoopy plate and utensils for Christmas, but it would probably make matters worse.

Prescription

Most of your work with the Blamer will consist of preparation activities. At work when you are dealing with a Blamer who makes you the scapegoat for all his errors and poor performance, you need to take notes while he talks and read the notes back to him before you make a move. Keep your special "note" journal in a highly visible spot on your desk so that the Blamer gets used to seeing it. It will become a reminder that even though being accountable gives him cramps, he'd better get used to it. To make sure that you set the stage for putting the responsibility where it should go, ask a lot of open and closed questions (which you'll learn about in chapter 4) up front. This will help to eliminate any confusion and give you protection when the stuff starts hitting the fan.

If he says something critical like "You acted like a fool at dinner and if I lose the account, it's your fault," you can always answer, "Oh," or "Is that what you thought?" or "How would you have preferred I act?" or "When you want something specific from me, it would be helpful if you would let me know beforehand so that you and I might discuss it in as much detail as necessary."

If you choose to confront the Blamer when he is being critical, when he says, "You *would* say something like that," use a clarifying question (chapter 4). Answer, "That sounded like a dig. Is that what you intended?" Then deal with whatever answer you get. If he says yes, you say, "There's nothing I can do to respond to a dig. If you tell me specifically what you are referring to, I am willing to discuss it with you."

His belief is that he is too important to take responsibility for anything. That's why he blames you. Don't try to knock down his belief. When he begins to criticize, imagine that he's putting mud on a silver tray and handing it to you. Look at the mud on the tray and say to yourself, "Hmmmm, mud on a sterling silver tray. I don't want it, I don't need it, and I'm not going to pick it up." Just look at it. When the Blamer does his thing, instead of getting suckered into a battle, remain neutral. This takes practice, yet it can be done. If he criticizes you or judges you, so be it. In your mind, think, "Okay, I heard that. Now what?" Wait for him to speak again. Don't get defensive. Instead, get pensive. Watch, wait, and listen.

Dealing effectively with the Blamer, then, means positioning yourself so that you are in control of you and the information you are working with; it means being able to ask open and closed questions that will enable you to uncover information (proof) afterward. It also means being able to confront without being defensive, hostile, or emotional. These are all the skills you will find in chapter 4.

THE LOGIC PUSHER ◀

Description

The Logic Pusher is the guy who gets annoyed when, according to him, you try to clutter facts with feelings. He is truly inconvenienced by emotions and finds them messy, impossible, and irritating to deal with. He makes his case with data and that's all he cares about, and he uses his facts as weapons, a way to control you. He might be a Techno-weenie or a Number Nerd, and he's never met an authority or a statistic he didn't like. If you can't prove it to him, it just doesn't exist.

Pam experienced a classic Logic Pusher when she told her husband of ten years, "You never tell me that you love me," and he replied, without even looking up from his book, "I've been here for ten years, and I'm still here. What else do you want?"

Logic Pushers can be cold or they can be neutral, which is not as icy as cold but not warm and inviting either. Their worlds are black and white, all or nothing, yes or no. They have no patience for opinions, only for facts that can be substantiated. They believe their own facts much more than they believe yours, and they expect that as a woman and an overemotional being, you will probably be short on facts and long on irrational feelings and opinions. They can be shrewd and cunning, always looking for an angle, a way to justify their own beliefs.

Prescription

Whenever someone disagrees with Shel, my friend's husband, he makes his case, and then machine-guns them with questions. When I first met him, I was slightly taken back because I really felt like I was on a hot seat and had to defend myself. Then I got smart.

I decided to try a new approach, pulling him off course. You have to know Shel to really appreciate this; he is a person who is meticulous about everything, including his appearance, so this was the soft underbelly I decided to aim for. In the middle of one of his inquisitions, I suddenly looked him up and down and said, "Excuse me, Shel, I hate to ask you this, but have you put on a few pounds? Your cheeks look really cute now, they look like chipmunk cheeks." I couldn't have chosen better. After he denied it vehemently, reviewing his eating and exercise schedule with me in great detail, I looked at him in my most understanding way and said, "Of course, you haven't gained weight. I probably need new glasses.

Now, what were you asking me?"

It's all about using humor, in addition to skill. All I did was ask a question, and I completely changed the dynamics of the situation. By the way, he and I have become good friends, and I still tease him about his cheeks. When dealing with a Logic Pusher, when humor isn't the answer, you must do two things: First, control your emotions. You can have them, just don't expect him to acknowledge them. Second, do your homework. If he listens to logic, give him logic. Don't make emotional appeals. They are meaningless and will ultimately work against you in that he will discount you for having them in the first place. The more proof you can offer, the better. Anything in writing (documentation) would be helpful. Instead of saying, "This is how I feel about..." say, "This is what makes this situation important" and use words like "implications" and "impact." You can't out-logic a Logic Pusher. If he really starts chugging along, just step aside and let him run his course. Don't be intimidated and don't compromise your beliefs. Do use questions to make him give you the opportunity to poke holes in his pitch.

Let the Logic Pusher talk, and if you're so inclined, when he's finished say to him, "The information you gave me is very interesting. It's hard to grasp so much at once. Where can I read more about it on my own?" Make sure that you don't sound sarcastic when you say this.

Use visuals when you talk to him; body language is very important. For example, say, "I have three points to make regarding this issue," and then hold up three fingers and count off the issues as you bring them up.

Marta went to a conference where she was one of two women with seven men in a problem-solving simulation group. One of the men immediately took over, barking orders, and began making decisions based on numbers, financial information that the group had to work with. Whenever Marta made suggestions, he dismissed her and pointed back to the figures on the page.

Marta chose the right time and place, which we will discuss in chapter 5 ("Conflict Savvy"), and said, "Up until now, during our discussions about strategy, you dismissed what I said, interrupted me, and didn't really listen to my input. Here are some examples of what I'm talking about." After she cited the examples, she then proceeded to tell him how she wanted and had a right to be treated. She held her own, kept her focus on his behavior and what she had a right to in this situation, didn't sink to making personal attacks or insults, maintained direct eye contact, and finally wore him down. Marta refers to the situation as one in which she "tamed a bronco." She and her Logic Pusher actually developed a good working relationship over the next nine days.

When dealing with the Logic Pusher, don't throw the baby out with the bath water! Use him when you need research material or advice. If he's a Techno-weenie and a cook, when you need computer or car advice, invite yourself to dinner. It might be worth putting up with his lectures to get the information you need, and you'll get a great meal. Another bonus is that he will want to follow through on whatever he says he will do for you because he wants to look good. Take advantage of it. Ask him questions that he can relate to and answer easily, and let him feel good about himself and his knowledge. The following questions are two of my particular favorites:

"What do you see as the implications?"

"What would be the logical next step?"

After you've read the section on questions in chapter 4, prepare yourself immediately by making a list that you can use with Logic Pushers. It never hurts to get ready in advance.

When dealing with a Logic Pusher, keep your cool and detach yourself emotionally. I like to visualize the Logic Pusher as a big computer with a head (sporting a bad haircut), weird glasses, and flat feet with tennis shoes. This helps me keep my perspective. The Logic Pusher often comes across as very cold and uncaring, and your job is to stop expecting him to care so that you won't constantly be disappointed.

This is a difficult man who requires that you be ready with facts or moves. Questioning and feedback skills will serve you well here, as will knowing when to speak up and when to clam up (chapter 5).

THE BAITER-AND-SWITCHER ◀

Description

The Baiter-and-Switcher is the difficult man who uses your feelings as a weapon against you.

He'll pull you toward him in one emotionally seductive way or another, and the minute you surrender, he'll push you away. He maneuvers so that you do all the relationship work, and he takes all the credit. He looks like a caring person, he sounds like a caring person, but he's not a caring person. He's a fraud. He's a noncommunicator about real issues and the game he plays is Guess What I'm Thinking; Wrong, Guess Again. He's good at turning you on, then tuning you out.

That's how he controls you, by constantly changing the game and the rules—and what skill he displays doing it! This man is smooth. When he asks you how you feel, he does it in such a way that you really believe he wants to know, and he knows just how to phrase his questions and just how to look into your eyes so that he reaches your soul. That's why it's so chilling when, after you have let down your guard, he immediately switches off, dismisses you, and focuses on something totally different.

Most Baiter-and-Switchers are really good at removing your barriers, and at those infrequent times when they do encounter resistance, they have two or three stockpiled, soft-touch, Mr. Sensitivity stories they pull out and use to soften you up. And when you take the bait, they quickly change the tone of their dealings with you and put their stories away for the next time they want to penetrate your armor. Their trick is to make you feel comfortable; lull you into a false sense of security, trust, and acceptance; and then slam the door shut. You're trapped.

Dorothy's husband started the evening off being attentive and romantic; he said wonderful things, asking about her day and why she seemed a little down. When she answered that it wasn't important enough to discuss (which, by the way, is another self-deprecating thing that women do to erode their own importance and credibility), he pushed her to open up. When she began to reveal her true feelings and tell him how upset she was about something that had happened at work, his first reaction was "I can't believe you're making such a big deal about this." He then opened his newspaper and made her feel as if she'd stepped into an abyss. She felt embarrassed about having shown her true feelings, and she vowed never to open up again. But, of course, unless she changes the dynamics of her relationship with the Baiter-and-Switcher, she will open up again and get kicked in the stomach many more times.

Toni encountered a Baiter-and-Switcher at work. One day her boss came over to her and asked if everything was okay, because she didn't look like her usual self. When she told him that she was worried about her sick child, he told her to take the rest of the day off to take care of her. Two weeks later, he gave an important project that she was supposed to get to one of her coworkers. When she asked why, he told her it was because he couldn't count on her to be reliable; she didn't have her priorities straight.

Prescription

So what can you do with a difficult man like this? Simple. Don't take the bait. If you do take the bait, as soon as you realize it, resolve not to take the bait again—

ever! Don't walk around with the word *sucker* on your forehead. Every woman can make a mistake once, but twice, forget it! Your biggest mistake will be to see this guy as having potential because you've experienced his "soft" side. Baloney! He has no soft, feeling, or sensitive side, only a slimy underbelly. So don't confuse the two.

I have seen women waste their lives and careers on men like this and destroy who they are and their own self-esteem in the process. Don't get lured into the "maybe he'll change" web. This man is dangerous. He wants to tug at your strings and watch you jump and dance around. He wants to control you as he would a puppet. Don't let him get to your guts. He wants to sprinkle salt on them.

I have a strong bias against the Baiter-and-Switcher because he is more than just difficult, he is downright dishonest, and to me, there is no valid excuse for being that way. Baiter-and-Switchers also have other character-istics that make them doubly troubling. You may some-times encounter a Baiter-and-Switcher who is on the cusp of the Blamer, so be prepared. Claire still remembers an evening when George said to her: "You never want to share your feelings with me. You never tell me what's going on with you. You get crabby and I don't know why. You treat me badly, and I don't deserve it. Not only that, you don't treat anybody else as badly as you treat me."

He then sat on the couch with an expression that reminded her of a depressed basset hound. As soon as she started to soften, to explain her frustration, he began telling her that he was never to blame and that she was the one screwing up the relationship.

Claire knows that when she loses her temper, it is non-productive and makes things worse, and that it is much better when she asks open questions (chapter 4) to find out what he is upset about. If either of them gets too upset, she leaves the room, saying that she can't talk right now, and resumes the conversation ten or fifteen minutes later.

This is a good tack to use because it keeps you in control or helps you regain it quickly if you've lost it. You'll learn more about it when we talk about positioning in chapter 5.

Be very careful when you deal with the Baiter-and-Switcher. Keep this guy at arm's length. No matter how charming and friendly he tries to get, draw a definite line in the relationship. It is too easy to start talking and opening up to him as you would a close friend, only to find that if you talk, you will pay, and pay, and pay. Guard yourself against being taken in by the Baiter-and-Switchers of the world. Be suspicious of men who are overcomplimentary, especially in front of other people.

If your difficult man is a Baiter-and-Switcher, as you read on, pay particular attention to the section on how to adjust your attitude (chapter 3). Decide whether it is worth it to you to speak up or clam up (chapter 5). If speaking up is your choice, don't talk feelings, because to this difficult man feelings mean vulnerability, and he salivates at the thought of getting his hooks into you. Talk about behavior, interpretations, and results. Cut your emotional investment; cancel it, in fact, since this difficult man is going nowhere in the feeling department. Choose a confrontation technique (chapter 4) that you feel comfortable with and stick to it. Study, practice, and learn to use open questions to get him to tell you more about his agenda. You may want to throw in a little guilt (chapter 5); it can't hurt. As my friend Amy was fond of saying, "What's wrong with guilt? It works."

● THE ADMIRATION HOUNDS

Difficult men motivated by admiration include the Executive, the Stud, and the Self-proclaimed Expert. These presidents of their own fan clubs have the basic attitude that they are really hot and that you are not, and they want you to agree with this assessment, loudly, openly, and often. Their basic stance is that women are put on this earth to make them look good. They expect no competition from you, and they want you to defer to them in the attention department.

THE EXECUTIVE ◀

Description

The Executive is often an empire builder who wants you as a subject. At work, he takes the best assignments and gives you the dregs. At home, he is king, and you are supposed to put his wants and needs first. His belief is that he's too important to do the work; he expects you to do it for him. He's convinced that he deserves the best and that you deserve to give it to him.

Hope's boss made a mistake with a customer and told Hope to write a letter of apology to the customer and sign her name, explaining that it would look bad for the company if someone at his level was wrong, but that no one would be surprised if she was. The arrogance of this difficult man! The nerve! The chutzpah!

These men, ridiculous as they are in the self-inflated ego department, are also dangerous because of their condescending behavior. And if there's one thing that gets my complete attention, it's a condescending difficult man.

A lot of Executives started from nothing and built their new images to their own exact specifications. Many think they are above everything and everybody else. They want to be seen as having been born with the proverbial silver spoon in their mouths. They want women to revere them, and if you, as a woman, are not interested in revering, this difficult man either isn't interested in you or will work on you until you come around to his way of thinking.

When confronted about something he's done, he refuses to acknowledge that there's a problem with him. He needs to have someone obey him in order to feel important. He wants to be put on a pedestal, admired, and respected. He really thinks that he is above everybody else, especially you if you're a woman. He expects you to handle all the details, clean up after him, and make him look as impressive as he really thinks he is. Often, when Executives meet you, they love who you are. They say, "You're outgoing, you're assertive, and you're pretty. You make me laugh, and you're smart." Then, as the relationship progresses, they start to criticize the same qualities they loved you for in the beginning, because they're afraid that someone else will want you, that you'll leave them, and they'll look bad.

Prescription

Since the Executive wants attention, give him attention. If he has a big ego, feed his ego, get it over with, watch him calm down, and move on. You have to clarify your intent with an Executive. If it's to knock him down a peg or two, you're on the wrong track. Your job is to concentrate on maintaining control of yourself, not him. If he gives you the bum part of a job, talk about requiring continuity to complete the task so that it comes out of his department up to his usual high standards. Talk about him as your coach and mentor and express how much his senior savvy helps you do things well. Snow the sucker.

This kind of guy exercises control by keeping you in a deferential position. If up until now you have been resisting, confuse him by treating him like an executive so that you can maneuver and get what you want.

This is a good difficult man to barter with. Offer to do something extra for him that you know he wants (it can't be illegal, immoral, unethical, sexual, or fattening) and put in a proviso for you. Be direct with an Executive if you think he is trying to use you or make you look bad. Use one of the confrontation techniques we're going to discuss (chapter 4): describe what you see or hear; give him your interpretation and ask for an explanation; then close your mouth, tightly, and don't get hooked into filling silent space.

At home, clearly define your boundaries. "I know you don't like to do the dishes. It is a waste of your time. That's why I thought you'd enjoy vacuuming. It requires much more skill, and you don't run into the furniture or break things the way I do. You're much better coordinated."

Abby's boss, Jim, sees himself as an open, fair, easy-to-approach, nonsexist, nonjudgmental person. In fact, he is the exact opposite. He is very stubborn, and when he makes up his mind about an issue, there is very little she can do to get him to look at another side of it. He has been known to say that "a woman couldn't handle this type of job." Although he says that he is approachable, when she acts friendly he withdraws into his pompous mode. His body language changes and lets her know she hasn't been deferential enough.

Abby deals with Jim by being personable, not personal. She has learned always to show that she knows that he is important, and in return, he does favors for her and engages her as a confidante.

If you want to get things from the Executive, praise him and reinforce what he does and says. Don't be critical of him, because he sees no middle ground. To him, you're either with him or against him, so watch yourself. The Executive can be vindictive, because he is very competitive. He has no intention of sacrificing his status for you or your needs. You are expendable if you don't add to his aura. Make him feel good about himself and work your agenda around him.

THE STUD ◀

Description

The Stud shuffles women like a deck of cards, always trying to get a better hand. When it comes to getting dressed to go out, he spends more time getting ready than you do. He's sure that no woman has ever faked it with him. He never passes a mirror or a plate-glass window without giving himself an admiring glance.

The Stud can be a fun difficult guy to deal with. A Stud can be a player (major womanizer), a pretty-boy (the guy who primps and preens), or a macho man (the caveman of the lineup). He'll flex his pecs at the drop of a hat. He's into himself and his body. He thinks he's terrific and wants you to think so too. He is arrogant, self-centered, self-consumed, and usually very, very boring to be around. There's only one way to do things—*his* way—and he thinks that you should be grateful to have the opportunity to do anything related to him.

Deanna, a woman with children in their twenties, laughed when she recounted a situation she had with a guy in his early twenties who kept asking her out. "When I looked at him," she said, "I imagined 'son' written across his T-shirt. When I said, 'No, thank you, I don't want to date you; you're too young,' he replied, 'You've gotta be kidding. You should be flattered that a guy like me would even want to date you'." Arrogant, studly behavior? Definitely, yes: self-absorption and gall, earmarks of the classic Stud.

The Stud sees himself as a sort of Hercules; a mass of

muscles; strong, more than good-looking, drop-dead gorgeous. I've even seen some self-proclaimed Studs who thought they were all of the above. They were wearing hairpieces that looked like road kill and more gold chains on their flabby chests than Mr. T would be caught dead in. Some of these guys probably blow-dried the hair on their chests. It didn't matter, though. Nothing could help them.

Many women buy into the dream of needing to be with a serious hunklike man. They like to be with very good-looking men and ignore the fact that sometimes, even though the wrapping is great, the gift inside really isn't. A lot of women are disappointed to discover their own sons become studs, the very same type of man that they themselves try to avoid or are forced to deal with in other parts of their lives.

Betty's son had a very progressive upbringing. He left home to go to college and came back with some ultra caveman beliefs and behaviors. Betty wasn't thrilled when he looked at her and said, seriously, "Mother, you're the woman. Go into the kitchen and make me some lunch. I'm hungry." She told him that he knew where the kitchen was, to which he responded that making lunch was women's work. She laughed and didn't get up.

Betty's son was a Stud with a large smattering of Executive mixed in. Even though he was young, he had very clear macho behaviors, and they were different from any of the values and attitudes that she had tried to instill in him as he was growing up. Betty tried talking to him about his gender biases, and when she got sarcasm in return, she decided to give up trying to do brain surgery on him. Instead, she decided to just say no when he came on like Macho Man.

Prescription

How do you deal with a Stud? First of all, prepare to have a good time. Never expect honesty from these difficult men; they delude themselves and believe their own delusions, and since they aren't forthright with themselves, how can they ever be with you?

Many years ago, I went to a restaurant with a woman friend. While we were in the bar waiting for our table, a guy came up to me and started doing something that I always find fascinating: he began having a conversation with me while staring at his reflection in the mirror over the bar behind me. All the time he was talking to me, he was adjusting his shirt and his gold chain, smoothing his greasy hair, fixing his dip curl in the front, and peering down at me. (There wasn't any saliva dripping down his chin, but there could have been.) He started with, "So, young lady, I'll be nice and talk to you, since I see your girlfriend got lucky and left you." (Actually, she was in the bathroom.) Then, he asked, "What do you do?" "I teach," I answered, trying not to encourage the conversation. But he persisted, and his primping was starting to tick me off.

"What do you teach?" he probed. "I teach sexuality," I answered, smiling. "You teach what?" "I teach sexuality."

"I don't understand," he faltered. "What is it you

don't understand," I asked innocently, "what sexuality is, or that I teach it?"

As I said, have fun with the Stud.

It turned out that he wanted to make me squirm by asking a lot of suggestive questions about sex. Finally, when I was really bored with his testicular testing, I informed him that from my research (really, I have never done research in sex), I could tell by the shape of his ears that he would have sexual problems within the next few years. For some strange reason, he took off to the other end of the bar and left me alone.

Studs make themselves vulnerable because they are so dependent on us to feel studly. If you want your way with a Stud, feed his ego, give him positive reinforcement, then strike when the iron is hot. If he wants to prove his studliness, let him. Any guy who wants to prove that he is strong by single-handedly carrying my desk or refrigerator down the hall has my blessing. "Go for it, big guy," I say, and mean it.

For those times when the Stud is in particularly good form and you want a comeback with a bite to it and you have nothing to lose, you might enjoy a couple of the phrases that you will find in chapter 6, on backlash. I don't suggest using them as a steady diet, but there are some occasions that do lend themselves to that kind of action.

The Stud becomes obnoxious when he is a real womanizer. Sexist, chauvinistic behavior is very unattractive, and you can choose if and when to do something about it. Someone calling you "girl" may or may not be a big deal. Someone telling you that you can't do something as well as he can because you're a woman might not be quite as amusing. These guys have their self-esteem wrapped up in their crotches. Choose your battles carefully, using the different "conflict routes" coming up in chapter 5, and keep him off balance by using questions that are probing (chapter 4).

THE SELF-PROCLAIMED EXPERT ◀

Description

The Self-proclaimed Expert thinks he is just that, an expert. He has an opinion on everything. He is the human answer to the hot-air balloon. He's the best, the greatest, and the brightest. No matter what you've accomplished, he's done more. He knows it all, and you know nothing. He brags about everything he's done in life, from kindergarten on. He's a legend in his own mind. He's always right. He dominates every conversation and relates everything you say back to himself. He probably wouldn't mind a bit if you bowed slightly when he entered a room. He likes to think on your feet instead of on his. He won't hesitate to tell you the right way to do something. He's beyond reproach.

Carol works with a man named Ethan, who has an answer for everything. No matter what the subject of conversation, he is the supreme source of knowledge. If you are talking about law, he speaks with so much conviction that someone who didn't know him would think he had a law degree. If you're talking about medicine, he has all the answers and knows exactly what course of treatment you should follow. If you disagree with him, he is incensed. How dare you question his omniscience!

The Self-proclaimed Experts never see flaws when he looks in the mirror. He sees wisdom, knowledge, experience, and probably holiness. That's why he can't imagine any woman not feeling grateful for any shred of knowledge that he is willing to grace her with. While the Stud is the acme of physical perfection, this one is the height of mental prowess.

So you know the type: a big shot, a know-it-all, and an expert on everything. He puffs up and struts around like he's really hot stuff, or he sits back and is right all the time and controls by being wise. Because he wants to be recognized for being the best and the brightest, he has a need to be a superpower, which means that he wants you to defer to him. He wants admiration, uses intimidation, and likes to be in charge of everything so that he can get the credit for it, and of course, he takes credit even if he isn't in charge. He's very condescending, patronizing, and frustrating to deal with. The phrase "I don't know" is one he's never mouthed.

Prescription

Let the Self-proclaimed Expert take charge if you must, but don't make it too easy for him. Pay attention to what he says, then try to follow his orders and get him to help you because he is so smart and so competent. While the Executive wants to be served, keep in mind that the Self-proclaimed Expert has an ego that needs to be fed or he becomes cranky and annoying. Ask him to coach you, to guide you, and to share his wisdom with you. Tell him that he's an interesting and important role model. He doesn't have to know that he's your idea of the one role model you never want to emulate.

Listen and acknowledge what he says, but don't confront him directly. Challenging him will only make things worse. Ask a lot of clarifying questions, combining open and closed (chapter 4). Get him to do the work for you or at least to plan it out. Pick his brain for as many ideas as you can. If you do need to disagree, make sure you do it with solid information. If he is convinced that his way is better, and he is resisting yours, say something like, "I am excited about working hard to enhance your ideas," or "People will go crazy with joy when they see the next level you'll have taken this to."

Again, your goal is to deal with him and get what you want, not change him. Always keep that in mind. Don't lose your focus.

You can cash in on the Self-proclaimed Expert's need to be admired not only by getting him to do a lot of your work but by getting him to take overall responsibility for projects. If he likes the limelight, give it to him when you know that it would be highly risky for you to take it without his support.

If he does help you out, don't be too grateful. Acknowledge his action and move on.

If you let the Self-proclaimed Expert know that you don't admire him, he'll probably go away. If that's what you want, great. But if you need him, remember to feed his all-knowing ego. If you don't fawn over him, or if you tell him straight that you don't like what he does or that you don't respect him as an informed person, he will usually cut off the relationship, because he can't stand it when he's not treated like a sage. So be careful. Don't cut him loose just because he ticks you off.

If you have an investment in the relationship (for example, if he's your boss), you can protect yourself by praising him, and the thicker you pour it on, the better. Ask him to share his knowledge and expertise with you. Ask for his advice. Request that he give you the benefit of his vast experience and let you run some ideas by him for his input. At work, the Self-proclaimed Expert bases his decisions about how to deal with you and how generous to be on how much he thinks you like and revere them. If he thinks you like and revere him a lot, he'll do anything for you. Don't worry about being right or being deserving in order to get what you want. He sees himself as a fountain of information; turn on the spigot and let him spew.

You can use him to do things that you don't want to do, or you can keep him dangling by varying the amount of reverence you give them. If you want to get really good at doling it out, check the section on "Confronting and Giving Feedback" in chapter 4. You'll get a lot of good ideas about how to shovel it with style.

●THE NURTURE NEEDERS

The Commitment Phobic, the Wimp, and Mama's Precious are difficult men motivated by the need to be nurtured or taken care of. They are similar to those who need admiration and are easier to deal with than those motivated by the need for power. Their basic stance is that they are helpless victims who need you to acknowledge how difficult life is for them and how much they suffer. They want women to recognize the sacrifices they make and to understand that they are fragile and sensitive. They don't want to be hurt; they want to be protected and insulated; and they certainly don't want to be challenged. These are the guys who want to show up in life and have someone else lead them through it, and if that someone is you, at home or at work, you are doing two jobs and getting paid for one.

THE COMMITMENT PHOBIC ◀

Description

The Commitment Phobic is like the black hole of emotional need. This difficult man doesn't want to have to give. He does want to take, and he controls you by needing more and more from you without ever giving anything back. I was reminded of how clever the Commitment Phobic can be when Charlene approached me at the end of a management training class and asked for help in dealing with her significant other of six years, a true Commitment Phobic. "He tells me that he loves me and that he wants to spend his life with me, and when I ask him when this arrangement will begin, he says, "Don't pressure me. If you love me, you'll accept me and let me do this in my own time."

Now, if Charlene asked you for advice, what would you tell her? That's what I said, too. This man will not commit. Forget it and move on. Will she do it? Maybe, after she's been strung along for another year or two. Too many women refuse to recognize commitment phobia. They deny that it's happening or that they can't do much about it. They think that the Commitment Phobic will be different and come around with them.

The Commitment Phobic is an expert at stringing you along, and it can be exhausting to deal with him. At work, he won't be pinned down. You want a delivery date or the date of completion of a project? Getting one is like pulling teeth, and then he still doesn't follow through. Some Commitment Phobics are perfectionists, and their behavior is a way of saying that nothing will ever be right enough, so why even try? It is a convenient curtain to hide behind.

For some strange reason, a lot of these men feel compelled to tell women they've just met socially that they aren't staying forever; and because they're so fearful, it is probably better for the women that they don't. That doesn't make their assertion any easier to swallow, however, since rejection is tough, regardless of who is doing it, especially if we lose our perspective and objectivity.

Commitment Phobics can drive you crazy with their indecisiveness. Not to say that they aren't also charming, because they are, and it is this that makes them even more frustrating. Women tend to "if only" more about these difficult men because they appear to get so close to action, and then—whoooosh! they're gone. Avoidance is their middle name. Women who have a strong need to help other people are the best targets of these men, and these men want to make women happy because they want women to like them. It is actually a vicious circle that we have going on here, and it is usually the woman who has to be willing to end the ride.

Prescription

How do you deal with a Commitment Phobic? Very slowly and deliberately, to be sure. You have to contract with him up front for small things, since he is totally overwhelmed by anything big. He is so controlling when he begins to back away that you have to guard against letting him suck the life out of you.

Don't try to bring about any kind of rapid or even average change with these men, because change makes them nervous. They like things the way they are because they feel more in control that way.

Joline had a chance to test her conflict savvy (chapter 5) and her problem-solving when she went out on a blind date with a man who seemed very interesting and fun to be with. She didn't make any assumptions, however, and decided to let him take the lead. At first, she was horrified, and then she was amused that on their second date, while having coffee, he looked at her with the utmost seriousness and said, "I don't want to hurt you. I know that you are going to really fall for me, but I've just come off of a bad relationship experience and I won't be able to give you what you want. I can't give you all of me, and I know you'll be devastated. I want to keep seeing you, but I don't want you ever to expect me to settle down or have a really serious relationship. I've been badly burned, and it has ruined me for other women."

Joline didn't know whether to laugh, applaud, or leave. What would you have done? She stayed and she played it cool. She didn't have to play hard to get because she *was* hard to get. Had he asked her, he would have found out that she wasn't humming "Here Comes the Bride" when he rang her doorbell. She had no expectations that this would turn into anything, so it really didn't matter. Emotionally, she had no feelings of ownership. By the way, after a few years, they actually did get married and have remained so; and by the end, it was his idea. You just never know.

But not all Commitment Phobics are salvageable. As we saw with Charlene, some are disasters from the word "go," and that's what you should do.

What else do you do with a Commitment Phobic? Find out what is at the root of his unwillingness to commit. Is it based upon fact, feeling, past experience, or what? You need to make it easy for him to tell you the truth. Learn to ask questions without a heavy dose of emotionalism, empathy, or guilt. Just ask your questions. For example: "If you did decide to get married, what are two or three of the changes you think it would make in your day-to-day life?" Or, "If you did commit to a completion date for this project, what problems do you think might arise that would make meeting the deadline difficult for you?" You can also ask him a very direct, closed question, "What will it take for you to commit?" and when he answers, follow up with open questions to learn more about what he is basing his answers on.

Another method for dealing with Commitment Phobics is to use questions that give them forced choices, such as "Are you willing to just attend the meeting or do a presentation at the meeting?" Or, "Are you more interested in a casual relationship or a long-term involvement?" This is also a good time to use the problem-solving model coming up in chapter 4; the reason being that you can learn more about the barriers they are putting up in their mind and how to take them down, one at a time.

Give your Commitment Phobic a lot of positive reinforcement when he makes even the smallest commitment and keeps it. Don't gush so much that he has to dig himself out from under, but do be direct, up, and complimentary in specific terms. "You said you'd go to this event with me, and you did. It means a lot to me. Thank you."

Use what you will learn about body language in chapter 4 when dealing with a Commitment Phobic, and establish direct eye contact. Don't stare or glare, but don't divert your eyes either. Use a moderate tone of voice; don't whine or demand, and make no assumptions. Since the Commitment Phobic wants to be taken care of, he also responds well to a lot of the emotions wasted on the Powermonger or Admiration Hound. It is often helpful to tell him how you feel as a result of his behavior. Don't use guilt if you can help it, because he's likely to bolt from the pressure.

THE WIMP ◀

Description

The Wimp is the ostrich of the lineup. Since he likes to keep his head in the sand, his rear end is exposed and up in the air a lot; a clear invitation to kick him around.

The fact that he prefers to hide in a bucket of sand, though, doesn't mean you should give it to him. This guy is a big chicken. The thought of making a tough decision gives him cramps. He crumbles under pressure and is often known to whine and squirm. He does a stellar imitation of a doormat.

Wimps can be slugs as well, the type of difficult man who sits around so much that after a while you are convinced he has grown roots. As a slug, he has no energy or desire to think, say, or do anything. The world happens without him, and that's just the way he likes it. He's good at getting other people to do things for him so that he doesn't have to do anything for himself. He's different from the Executive, however, because he feels and communicates that he is not worthy. He wants to feel safe and secure, a condition he perpetuates by resisting most changes. He denies having strong feelings because he doesn't want to have to do anything about them. He wants people to accept him and show him that they do by not forcing him to assert himself.

When forced to do anything, he becomes a skilled procrastinator, his theory being that if he waits long enough, whatever you wanted him to do will no longer be necessary or important. This ploy often works, since women often just give up on the men and do it themselves.

The Wimp wants to be pampered, nurtured, and taken care of, not unlike a child, and if he can't have that, he wants to be left alone. When children need an out, they often cop to saying, "My mother says I can't," even if they haven't ever asked her. It is a safe way to set and keep limits. Keep this behavior in mind when you are dealing with a Wimp, because like a child, he doesn't have the courage to say, flat out, "I don't want to." Instead, he worms, weasels, stalls, and zones out—anything to change the channel so you'll stop pressuring him.

How do you recognize a real Wimp? He's never the bad guy. Somebody else is always to blame. If he's the manager, he says things to his people like "I hate to do this. I don't agree with it, but my boss says we have to." He automatically assumes a victim stance.

John, an accountant, is afraid to tell clients the job will cost more than was originally discussed. He waits until the end and then surprises the client. He says, "You owe us another $100,000." When the client gets upset, he becomes even more wimpy and retreats even further. The client gets angry; John feels like a victim and decides that he can't win. He gives himself permission to stop trying, and someone else has to bail him out.

Prescription

There is not that much you can do with these difficult men. You can engage them, bypass them, or manip-
ulate them. You do have to watch that they don't set you
up by "yessing" you and building false expectations
about that which they will or will not deliver. And at
work, don't expect them to go to bat for you.

If your boss is a Wimp, and you want him to ask his
boss to approve a raise for you, don't hold your breath.
The only chance you have is if you coach him through it
and somehow convince him that doing this for you
would be the lesser of two evils. Wimps look for outlets
for the frustration they don't usually allow themselves to
release. They sometimes act irrationally just to release
steam. Decide when to speak up and when to clam up
(chapter 5). Be prepared to clean up any mess they make
if their action involves you, because they'll retreat soon
after they've acted out. Pay attention to who his advice-
givers are and try to be one of them. If you can't make
the inner circle, at least try to influence those who do.
Don't waste your time on the Wimp, unless you know
you can control his behavior.

If the Wimp is your significant other, keep this in
mind: once a wimp, almost always a wimp. The Wimp
will always be an extension of you; if you are a powerful
person, he will piggyback on your success and blame you
for any failures. Resist the urge to mother the Wimp.
You can be helpful, but only if you set clear limits, and
always try to get to the Wimp first and last so that the
other people trying to influence him in between won't be
able to.

Strong women often don't bother with Wimps. They just work around or go over them. This intimidates the Wimps even more, and they become even more Wimp-like, or they agree to do things and then never get them done.

Women marry Wimps for different reasons. Sometimes it's because they themselves have no self-confidence. Sometimes it's just because they want to be with an easygoing, noncombative person, not realizing that "noncombative" really spells "jellyfish." And sometimes it's because they are very strong and they want to be with someone they can control.

When insecure women develop self-confidence or when strong women get tired of getting nothing in return, they may decide that it's time to redefine their relationship with the Wimp so that they don't run the risk of being bored.

Wimps don't stand up for themselves, and this can be frustrating. The best way to deal with them is not to challenge them but to build a nonthreatening relationship in which they don't have to compete.

Wimps need to feel connected to you. Wimps like to bond and make personal contact. Even if they are armchair jockeys who do nothing more than ride the remote because they are hiding from the world, be as personable as you can to make them feel more secure. Ask for their ideas and their input (during commercials for starters, if necessary). Make them feel special. Build them up now so that you can make requests of them later. This is a gradual process, so don't go in piling it on all at once. Pace yourself. Try a compliment or acknowledgment of something they've done and watch their reaction. Ask questions (chapter 4):

> *"The purple cover is great! What made you*
> *decide to try a purple cover on your report*
> *this time?"*

Ask them to do small things, and give them as much time as possible to do them. Check in with them regularly, and give them permission to have problems. Say things like "Nothing ever goes totally smoothly for anyone." Give them an easy question to answer: "What are some of the things that are going well?" Then add a more focused question: "What are some of the things not going so well?" You will be encouraging them to tell you by giving them permission to say anything at all. Some difficult men are the "get right to the point" type. Wimps are not. They need to talk over lunch or coffee. They need to be pumped up and stroked. Talk about the kind of relationship they'd like with you and express your enthusiasm about getting to know them better. Remember that an ostrich takes its head out of the sand only if it is sure there isn't someone with an axe looking over its shoulder. To them, life just isn't fair, and there is always something wrong. Don't add to their grief; be the sun shining through their dark clouds.

A lot of men appear wimpy on the outside but are really passive-aggressive on the inside. They'll sit back and not say anything, listen and take it all in, and then use the information they've gleaned in negative, underhanded ways. Watch for hidden agendas with men who are seemingly Wimps. They could be closet Blamers, and if they are, go back and reread the prescription section for Blamers.

If Wimps are your difficult men, pay particular attention to the feedback, questioning, and timing techniques in the next two chapters.

MAMA'S PRECIOUS ◀

Description

Now, we come to Mama's Precious, the difficult man who, like Peter Pan, won't grow up. Behaving as an adult would mean having to accept responsibility and own up to his own wants, needs, feelings, and opinions. He wants you to take care of him, maybe pay all of his bills, stop making demands, and even wipe his nose (figuratively speaking). He expects you to run interference for him, keep him safe, and if you really want to please him, do his laundry.

Through the magic of an expandable umbilical cord, he is still very tied to his mother. Even though he may be 20, 30, 40, or 50, he has never really left home. What's he looking for is the ultimate bosom to nuzzle in, and nobody else's can live up to his mother's bosom. They just don't feel the same.

Kathy married Martin, who loved his mother's cooking and wanted Kathy to cook exactly the same way. A few weeks after their wedding, when Martin told Kathy how much he liked vegetable soup, she spent hours making it. When Martin got home, she proudly put the soup in front of him and waited eagerly for him to taste it. Horrified, she watched as he pushed the vegetables around the bowl with his spoon and said, "Why didn't you strain it? I hate to eat pieces of vegetables. My mother always strains my soup for me." Kathy was aghast. "Will this make the vegetables small enough?" she asked as she dumped the entire pot down the garbage disposal and flipped the "on" switch. Okay, maybe her reaction was a little extreme, but it did show that she had style and a certain flair! Sometimes, you get a Mama's Precious who grew up being told what to do and now wants to tell you what to do.

What are some of the danger signs?

1. He starts sentences with "My mother wants" instead of asking you, "Do you want...?"

2. He doesn't want to hurt *her* feelings; for example, he says it's okay if she bakes cookies and stops by without calling first to deliver them because they're his favorite, she worked so hard, and he wouldn't want to hurt her feelings. Your feelings? Why they're not important here at all. He doesn't even know that you have feelings.

3. When his mother starts telling you what to do because you're with him and you realize you're really having a relationship with two people— the mother and the son—you know you are in trouble.

The bad news is that on one hand, Mama's Precious may be a very nice person who will be attracted to you because you remind him of his mother, and on the other hand, he will be repelled by you for the very same reason. He may very well have a passive-aggressive streak rooted in the fact that you are strong and he is still dealing (unsuccessfully) with his mother as a strong and dominating force in his life. He might have a lot of unresolved issues with his mother, and you get to experience the brunt of them. He might do some Baiter-and-Switcher maneuvers, like opening up the communication channel just a bit and then switching stations when you say something he doesn't want to hear.

Prescription

When dealing with Mama's Precious, be very aware that even if Mama died, she'd still be very much alive for him, and it wouldn't make much difference in the way he relates to women. You need to make this difficult man see that he has something to offer not just his mother but the rest of the world as well. If you are married to him, you have to work on making it possible for him to build his self-esteem. You also have to set some boundaries. You would do well to use some of the confrontation and feedback tools coming up in chapter 4. This guy needs all the help he can get. If you are involved with a Mama's Precious, take special note of the responses to putdowns you'll find in chapter 6.

So now you've seen them, difficult men in all their glory. Some are dangerous; others can be fun to deal with because their behavior is actually quite ridiculous. They are all challenging, however, especially when they are in power positions or are trying to control you.

The next step is to learn about how your attitudes may be holding you back from dealing effectively with these difficult men, and how easy it can be for you to adjust your attitude and begin to turn these difficult relationships around.

The
Party Is Over
(for Difficult Men)

Dealing with people, and especially difficult-men people, is a matter of trial and error (mostly error). Think of yourself as being on a journey that has endless possibilities. We know that you are a good person (okay, maybe not in the perfect or stellar range all the time, but at least good). We know that you don't intentionally try to get difficult men to take advantage of you or treat you shabbily. We know that many men have traditionally treated women as second-class citizens, and we know that our world still reinforces this behavior. But Rome wasn't built in a day and neither will your new set of skills be.

As women, we need to be willing to let men know that what they're doing isn't okay—that we understand it, we see through it, and we're above it. In this chapter, we'll talk about how a change in attitude can begin to change your way of relating to your difficult men. To me, this is where the fun begins!

Maybe you're not as enthusiastic as I am and you've been asking yourself, "Why me? Why do I have to be the one to carry the burden of getting difficult men to stop being difficult when they deal with me? Why won't they just grow up—again, and better this time? Why can't they just change by themselves?" Since I have seen the future and it still has difficult men in it, we might as well just accept the fact that they won't and move on. All people can be difficult, and men present a particular challenge largely because of the testosterone factor that we talked about in chapter 1.

● TAKE STOCK OF YOUR BAD HABITS

Do you want to level the playing field? (It's about time we had at least one sports analogy.) If you do, it's up to you to do some homework about some of your habits first.

Bad habits are interesting things to consider. How do we get them? It seems as though we grow them, they multiply without our even being aware of it, and before we know it we are stuck in the same old patterns.

Habits are not easy things to break. I myself still have to curb the impulse to reach for a very large bag of peanut M & M's when I am in a stressful situation. The one thing that helps me not reach for them is the picture that I keep of myself, taken after I had indulged in several bags.

Up until now, you may have been merely coping with difficult men, repeating behaviors that you have learned, whether they were effective or not. There is good news, however; as soon as you become aware of your bad habits, you can do something about them. So take some time now to review this list of bad habits to which most women can relate all too well. Be honest with yourself and answer truthfully. Think of this as a self-awareness quiz to help you recognize what you do when dealing with difficult men.

When you are dealing with difficult men, do you:

1. Automatically take a subservient position? Y

2. Say to yourself, "I'm probably overreacting?" y

3. Immediately assume a mothering role? Y

4. Convince yourself that if you did confront, you'd probably fall apart? Y

5. Become too aggressive? Y

6. Constantly decide that it's not worth it? Y

7. Ignore the cues that tell you it's time to back off? Y

8. Tell yourself that you're being too sensitive? Y

9. Worry that other people will blame you for any upheaval? Y

10. Immediately feel the need to walk all over them? Y

11. Worry about them not liking you? Y

12. Go for the cheap shot, because something is Y better than nothing?

13. Wish that you could grow facial and chest hair Y to fit in with the guys?

14. Act personal, instead of personable? Y

15. Tell them off on a regular basis? V

16. Never ask for what you want? Y

17. Use crying to soften them up? Y

18. Run hot and cold? Y

19. Share the reasons for your mood swings with anyone who'll listen? Y

20. Act like a victim when you don't get your way? Y

21. Ignore difficult male behavior, hoping it will go away by itself? Y

22. Wait so long to deal with something that you let it blow up out of proportion? Y

23. Keep hoping that difficult men will see the error of their ways without your having to confront them? Y

24. Use sex as your ultimate weapon? N

Did any of your answers come as a surprise to you? Were you aware of what you have been doing with difficult men? As women, most of us can relate to many of these habits because of our upbringing.

There is an expression that I have heard many times from many different sources: "The way you were raised is your parents' fault. If you stay that way, it's your own." In other words, you have choices. You can stick with and hide behind these bad habits, or you can refine them to better reflect who you are now and who you want to be. As you go through this book, the tools and techniques you will read about will act as replacement parts; so, for instance, instead of acting like a victim when you don't get your way (number 20), you'll be able to realign your reactions and do some strategic planning. You'll tell yourself that even though you didn't get your way this time, next time you'll be ready with a new attitude, a new approach, and some hot new maneuvers.

Of course, it must be said that if we were talking about men, a lot of these habits would not be seen as bad, which makes it even more important *never* to forget that there is a double standard, even today!

When we can be honest with ourselves and acknowledge that we have these bad habits, we will already be on the road to recovery, even though most of us know that merely to acknowledge something does almost nothing to actually change it. For this, we need to make the commitment to work on changing ourselves by changing what we do.

Which brings us to the first change: stepping out of our comfort zones, where our bad habits reside. Bad habits are comfort-zone keepers. They lull us into believing that just because something is familiar, it is helpful.

Not true. Just because "we've always done it this way" doesn't make it the best way to go. Let's take an example.

Perhaps you've gotten really good at number 16 on the bad habits list, telling people off on a regular basis. I know, this can feel very, very good at the time you do it, not unlike that first warm, smooth sensation of soft, rich chocolate melting on your tongue; but chocolate makes you fat, and telling difficult men off makes them even more determined to make your life miserable. If you tell difficult men off because you let yourself get to the boiling point instead of dealing with their difficult behavior one incident at a time, you'll never win the difficult-men war.

● CHOOSE TO BE ON TOP FOR A CHANGE

One of the biggest mistakes that women make is to treat problems with difficult men differently from the way they treat most other problems. As a management consultant, when I work with high-level executives who are having difficulty with other people in the organization, I teach them to begin by asking themselves and answering the following questions:

1. How would you define the problem?

2. Are you willing to work on it?

3. What would it look like "fixed"?

4. Are your expectations realistic?

These questions help set the tone for keeping your position on top. Being on top means planning instead of reacting. It means observing instead of feeling victimized. It means making choices based on information and gut feelings. But you've got to be willing to stop and take the time to do this—and to listen to your answers.

Norma applied this question-and-answer technique in a recent experience. As a child and then as a young woman, she had little self-confidence. But after her divorce, she took personal-development classes in assertiveness training, and as a result of this tremendous infusion of information and support, she went to the opposite end of the spectrum. For a while, she admits she could have put a "Bitches R Us" sign on her forehead and everyone would have agreed. Instead of defining a problem, finding out whether or not people were willing to work on it, visualizing it fixed, and making sure her expectations weren't unrealistic, she attacked.

To say that men would grip their chairs after she opened her mouth would be an understatement. She learned this by judging men's reactions to her when she came on too strong, too soon. This was particularly apparent once in a presentation that she was making for a men's professional association. In front of 200 men, one man stood up and told her that she was sounding "very bitchy." The room became so quiet, you could have heard a condom drop. All eyes were either on her or looking down. She couldn't believe it, even though he was probably right about her demeanor. It was embarrassing and humiliating, and she was ticked! After the shock wore off, she thought about how to respond.

Let me take you through her thought processes.

At first, she wanted to "thank him for the testosterone moment," then she wanted to ask him if his cave was air-conditioned. It also occurred to her to ask if anybody had an apple she could put in his mouth. Okay, she also wanted to ask him if he was uneducated or just very stupid. And, you guessed it, she wanted to ask him if premature talking was his only premature problem.

She finally decided to smile and say, "Thank you. I appreciate your honesty. I am strong, and sometimes it shows more than necessary." More silence, and then applause. She had turned other men in the group into her allies. The audience was hers, and there was no more heckling.

Being on top doesn't mean being more sarcastic than he is. It doesn't necessarily mean saying things like "Someone like you *would* say something like that." It doesn't even mean insulting a difficult man by saying, "You don't sweat much for such a large person." It means changing your perspective and adjusting your behavior so that you feel strong, upright, and powerful. Norma did this by clarifying exactly what the problem was, deciding that she was willing to address it, allowing herself to fantasize, and then pulling hersef back to reality.

Take a moment to look around the room you are sitting in right now; from your vantage point, it looks one way. Stand on a chair and you will see a very different sight. Kneel on the floor and the room changes again. The view you get from standing on the chair gives you a broader perspective that is more expansive. Plain and simple, things look different from up there on top.

● STOP SHOULDING
ON YOURSELF

Several years ago, I sat in on a meeting with Helene, a new client, during which she and three other department heads were discussing how to divide up a new office site. This person whom I was to begin coaching after the meeting, the only woman in the group, said nothing as one man after another selected all the offices that had windows and left one dark room that resembled a closet and three cubicles for my client and her staff. After the meeting, I asked her how satisfied she was with the final outcome, and she said that she was angry, disgusted, and disappointed. She hated the office space that she and her staff would be forced to occupy. She thought that her feelings should have been considered. It never occurred to her that in order to consider her feelings and take them seriously, other people had to know what they were. She spent the next week "shoulding" on herself and the other three department heads: "I should have gotten more." "They should have thought about my needs." "They should have asked me what I wanted." "They shouldn't have been so selfish and pushy."

I pointed out that these men were difficult because she allowed them to be. They did what worked for them since she had said nothing and had never let them know their actions were not what she wanted. She could have stated her wishes, disagreed with their plan, and negotiated for what she wanted. The other men (a) were not mind readers, (b) experienced no resistance so went full steam ahead with what they wanted, and (c) probably congratulated themselves on pulling one over on her. She kept on saying to me, "Well, it wasn't worth fighting about." What she was doing was depriving herself of what she wanted by blaming the situation on them, and the three difficult men didn't even have to be nasty or pushy. She gave herself a double whammy, because not only did she inflict the pain and have to deal with it, she then proceeded to blame herself for doing it. How exhausting, demoralizing, and counterproductive!

Shoulding on ourselves takes many forms. You know you're doing it when once again you find yourself having that same conversation with the steering wheel while you're driving home. Or you suddenly become aware that you are mutilating the produce in the grocery store when you stop to buy something for dinner after one of the meetings from hell made possible by a difficult man—or, worse, a group of difficult men.

Shoulding on ourselves means that we are using hindsight to reprimand ourselves for not having had the foresight to do or say something at a given time. This is a ridiculous thing to do because shoulding on ourselves is nothing more than a big waste of time.

Realistically, it is much more productive to say, "If I ever find myself in a situation like that again, what *could* I say and what *could* I do differently that *would* be more gratifying and constructive?" It might be that many of you hope that you will never have to repeat certain situations with difficult men in which you bombed, so you try to talk yourself out of planning for "coulds." At times like this, I feel compelled to remind you that when you're dealing with difficult men, forever just isn't as long as it used to be. Since it is easier to ask for forgiveness than permission, shoulding, or holding back, can be self-limiting, and not planning, or "coulding," will guarantee that you will be unable to increase your probability of success.

When we eliminate "I should have said" "I can't believe I said" "If only I had said" and "Why didn't I say" and substitute "What *could* I say to get what I want," and "What *would* I say to feel powerful, true to myself, and clear" we are finally starting to move in the right direction.

● STOP LIMITING, START BUILDING

In order to change the way men treat you, you have to be honest with yourself regarding the messages you may be putting out that are making you an easy target. What behaviors are you using that are undermining your equality potential?

Dealing with difficult men doesn't mean that you can have it all, however. A woman I know had been dating a man for several months. One night they were sitting in a restaurant, talking about which movie to see. She wanted to see one, and he, an Executive, wanted to see another. He stately flatly, "Since I'm the one who pays for everything, I get to decide what we do." She dropped her fork and swallowed her last bite of food, except for the piece that fell out when she unconsciously opened her mouth wide with disbelief and asked, "What did you just say?"

After the man repeated it exactly the way she had heard it, she looked at him in silence. At that moment, she considered leaving him with the check, but then realized that what she was hearing was his old programming talking and that he really believed what he was saying. So instead of cutting bait, she countered, "I have an idea. From now on, starting with this meal, we'll each pay for ourselves. That way, we'll be able to negotiate as equals about what we do." He was skeptical but agreed to go along. It worked. Granted, her free ride was over, but she gained a lot more in power and self-esteem than she had lost in dollars. P.S.: Wayne and I are now married, and we still split everything 50/50.

Not only is it important to know who you are, it is just as important to come to terms with what you do. The more information you have to work with, the more you can do what you need to do to create the changes you want.

Take a moment to answer these questions, and when you do, think about yourself at home and at work. Don't just think about your answers, but write them down.

1. If you were describing yourself to a woman, what would you say? Write the exact words that you would use. Consider how you would like to be seen by another woman.

2. Now, if you were describing yourself to a man, what would you say? Write the exact words that you would you use. Consider how you would like to be seen by a man.

Read what you've written. Are there some differences in your answers? Probably so. We tend to present ourselves differently to men and women. It is part of our conditioning, and most of us don't even realize what we are doing. What did you learn about yourself? What are your best characteristics? Did either one of your answers reflect these characteristics fully? Chances are, combining both answers would provide the best picture of who you are. Anything less is incomplete. We have to stop limiting ourselves when we show the world who we are, and we have to start building ourselves so that we can create the person we want to be.

To help you understand our self-defeating patterns, here's an example of how Jane answered the questions in one of my seminars.

To a man, she described herself as flexible, open, eager, and willing to learn, and to a woman, she said that she was dynamic, a fast learner, and smart. I hope that the difference is jumping off the page at you. Jane used stereotypically softer words to described herself to the man and stepped into the more stereotypically masculine domain for the woman. She diminished herself in the first case, and made herself seem weaker and less competent. This is one of those bad habits that we will talk more about breaking later in this chapter. Really think about this for a moment; it's an insidious tendency, and that's what makes it so destructive.

Do you tend to come across stronger in the relationships you have with women and weaker in your male relationships? A lot of women do. It is part of the training we talked about earlier. Or, you may be one of those women who seem to walk around with a chain saw when there is a man within 50 yards of them. This is not unusual. Many women believe that the best defense is a strong offense. Although this may be true, there is such a thing as going too far, being a little too intense, threatening too many crotch alterations.

Balance, that's what this is all about. Balance has to do with the way we behave based on the way we feel and our attitudes about ourselves. We can come across as too passive or too aggressive when we really need to be assertive. How do you choose the right place to be and the right mix of behaviors so that you feel true to yourself, and so that you are presenting a true picture to the man in your life, not inflating or deflating yourself and what you have to offer? Examine your attitudes.

● NICE GIRLS DO TALK BACK

Many of the tactics we will be talking about in the upcoming chapters may sound very different from those you usually resort to when dealing with difficult men, and as a result, your immediate reaction may be to toss them off, thinking, "I could never say that," or "I could never do that." Try not to let negativity or self-consciousness get in the way of your progress. If you are willing to take some small risks, you will learn that in fact you are very strong, much stronger than you have ever given yourself credit for. Every day will become like having a very good hair day with every single difficult man in your life, now and in the future.

And while you are using your new skills, each difficult man you test them on will see an outer image of control; so even if you're falling apart on the inside, it will be your secret. It won't show, and I know *I'm* certainly not going to tell them! Composure is an interesting phenomenon; it can look one way and feel another. When facing a difficult man, it is important to look as if you feel calm. You always have time to fall apart in private, later, and the more you try your new behaviors and get positive results, the faster your fear will subside and the less falling apart you'll do.

Nothing ruins my day faster than somebody taking advantage of me, and I know that I'm not alone in having this reaction. I hate it when people don't care about how I feel or what I want, and I get upset with myself for allowing it to happen, especially if it is a pattern that repeats itself. True, I sometimes get tired of being the one who has to establish the boundaries in a relationship, and it can be exhausting to have to ride shotgun for myself; but, hey, what's the alternative?

What can get discouraging to a lot of women is the recognition that for every difficult man whose behavior they neutralize, at least ten or twenty more lie in wait, and the supply is endless. There is a silver living to this cloud, however, if you think of this glut as a never-ending supply of difficult men on which to try all the new techniques you are about to learn.

As a friend of mine says, "Having a relationship with

a man that is give-and-take doesn't mean that we, as women, give and that men take."

What's the point of all this? The point is that nice girls really do talk back; they just do it nicely. Nice girls don't try to "out-man" difficult men by sounding rough and tough. Nice girls do talk to express rather than impress, and nice girls do this partly to keep difficult men watching the front door, while they slip in the side.

Let's cut to the chase. Nice girls do—and they do it with style!

The first step in changing your behavior toward difficult men is to adjust your attitude. The following list of actions will help. You may already practice some of them routinely. If so, that's great. It will give you time to think about and act on those that are new to you.

1. Recognize that your attitude is in your hands, and if you've been putting it in someone else's hands, now is the time to take it back, immediately.

2. See yourself the way you want to be, and always remember to start every single day with that healthy mental picture.

3. Stop worrying about what other people (difficult men-people) think. A lot of them hardly ever do think, and when they do, it's probably an underwhelming experience anyway.

4. Give yourself permission to make a fool of yourself. Perfection is boring, and when taken to extremes, is

referred to as obsessive. Enough energy wasted on
fixing what's not broken.

5.   Decide that it's okay to laugh at yourself. Look for
     the humor in tough situations with difficult men.
     Since the worst situations usually make the best sto-
     ries later (I am living proof of that), the more awk-
     ward experiences you have, the funnier you'll be at
     your next gathering.

6.   Decide that it's okay—no, *wonderful*—to ask for help
     from anyone you think can help you, male or
     female. One man sometimes knows exactly how to
     deal with another and is often willing to tell you
     when asked. Turn the enemy against itself, I always
     say, and adjust your "I am an island" behavior.

7.   Resolve to act the part and see what happens.
     When you try acting in control of yourself, you will
     find that you remain in control of yourself. What a
     feeling!

8.   Acknowledge your fear, feel your fear, but don't fail
     to try because of your fear.

Only you can control your attitude. The adjustment
switch belongs on the inside, not on the outside, where
you've been allowing difficult men to mess with it.

● POWER IS NOT A FOUR-LETTER WORD

Your attitude about yourself is closely related to how you feel about being powerful. In chapter 1, we talked about men and the myth of testicular power. We also talked about the fact that women are stereotyped as whiny and manipulative. Okay, I talked and you listened, but I think we agreed with the basic problem. Women often *are* whiny and manipulative—and men are too. But when men do it, we say they're cunning and strategically versatile.

Now it's time to talk about your power, because if you don't recognize it, you won't use it. Look in the mirror. Do you resemble your idea of how a powerful woman should look? Maybe you ought to back up a few steps and ask yourself what power really means and why you and so many other women have such a hard time owning and using it. What are your beliefs about power? Here is an opportunity to do a quick spot check. Keep in mind that power, like beauty, is in the eye of the beholder. My colleague, Melissa, is fond of emphasizing that the phrase "all that glitters is not gold" also relates to the perception of power—meaning that what one person sees as power, another may not.

Do you think each of the following statements is true or false:

1. **If you feel powerful, you'll look powerful.**

2. **She who has the loudest voice and quickest tongue will have the most power.**

3. Anyone can acquire power.

4. You can only be powerful if you are credible.

5. Power is something you can lose, and once you lose it, it is gone forever.

6. Men are automatically more powerful than women.

7. Information is power, and you can use it to control people and situations.

8. Confidence is power, and you can't be powerful without it.

9. Endurance is power: you need to last longer than anyone else.

10. Experience is power if the experience has been good.

11. Powerful people are automatically cold and insensitive to others.

As you read these statements about power, how did you respond?

Item 1: *True.* Our confidence usually shapes what people see, except when we use self-defeating behaviors or words that undermine our presence.

Item 2: *False.* A loud voice usually suggests that the woman is out of control, reacting emotionally instead of logically and playing too many cards too soon.

Item 3: *True.* Here are just a few of the sources of power:

Your position in a family or organization; your ability to negatively impact (really scare or threaten) another person; your ability to give people what they want, emotionally or otherwise; charisma, or a sparkling personality that another person finds charming and engaging; your possession of information that another person wants or needs; and last but not least, your personal connections to others (for example, you're tight with their boss).

How many of these sources of power do you currently possess, and are you taking advantage of them? Don't underestimate their usefulness in dealing with difficult men. Although they can all be invaluable, one problem many women have is the idea that using any kind of power is manipulative and therefore bad. This attitude, pounded into so many of us early on, accounts for our unwillingness to stand tall and be counted.

When Chris, a personal fitness trainer, walked into a room full of businessmen whom she was supposed to lead in a physical workout, she got to utilize a few sources of power. Listen to her recount what happened:

> *"Imagine me, six feet tall, blond, and—I'll say so myself—looking great, in tremendous physical condition, walking into the room wearing hot pink spandex workout clothes. I could just see all those guys thinking, "What is that?" and then fixating on the fact that I was blond and female and concluding, "Bimbette." It was really quite amazing to watch. When I announced it was time to get started,*

one guy actually stood up to work out with a lit cigar in his mouth. It took no time for me to demonstrate my strength. In front of his cronies and with a big smile on my face, before he even knew what hit him, I picked him up two feet off the ground and carried him to the door, where I deposited him and said, 'You can't smoke that thing in here.' I then proceeded to demonstrate the various activities the group would be doing and just for the heck of it, I bench-pressed a few hundred pounds. Needless to say, every man in the group behaved himself for the rest of that session, and nobody dared light a cigar or anything else for the rest of the week."

Chris did two things. First, we have to acknowledge that she did descend to the macho level and beat the guy at his own game. Not every woman can or wants to do that, but in this instance, it worked for her. She also used a combination of her experience, skill, and charisma to tame this group of difficult men. Their bimbette impression totally disappeared as soon as she lifted the cigar-smoking guy in the air. Her dry wit and willingness to play with them made it easy for them to look at her differently and enjoy her personality. She proved herself and made herself approachable with one quick interaction.

Item 4: *True.* Credibility really means that you have to be genuine, not necessarily the best or the brightest. If people think you're lying, they will not respond well.

Item 5: *False.* Everyday brings a new opportunity to try a different approach. Some days you might be more powerful, others less. There is no "forever" in the issues of power.

Item 6: *False.* What a bunch of bull! Women who are raised to feel and be competent and self-confident can match men step for step, move for move, and if a woman wasn't raised that way, as soon as she recognizes the void, she can raise herself retroactively.

Item 7: *True.* And although it is counterproductive, it must be acknowledged that withholding information is also a form of power. (So is withholding sex, but that's a topic for another discussion!)

Item 8: *False.* Women having been faking it for years (we're back to sex again), and the skills are definitely transferable. I like the idea of faking power better than faking orgasms, and if you're powerful, you don't have to fake anything, even during sex, because you feel good about yourself and are able to ask for what you want to get the real thing.

Item 9: *True.* But only if you can wear them down, and this sometimes incurs backlash, which is not so good.

Item 10: *True.* But only half the truth. Bad experience can also make you wiser and better prepared than anyone else.

Item 11: *False.* I suppose they can be, but the two issues are not related, and, in fact, powerful people often use their power to help others.

Has all this changed your mind about you and power? I hope so. I hope that you no longer believe that power comes from testosterone. Sure, it can, but it can also be estrogen-related, and as women, we are estrogen-intensive. Power does not have to be a male phenomenon. It can be had and enjoyed by all, so why not us?

In chapters 4 and 5, we will talk more about power moves that you can make and when you can make them; but in the meantime, ask yourself the following questions about power:

1. Do you use it?

2. What could you do right now to take advantage of what you've got and be more powerful?

3. When will you do a "try one"?

Come on, don't be afraid to commit to this. It will pay off.

● THEY DON'T HAVE TO LIKE IT

One of the most valuable bits of information I can share with you about changing your attitude and dealing with difficult men is something I learned one Saturday morning. Wayne, who is a wonderful person but definitely not a carpenter, walked into what would eventually be the kitchen in our new house, looked at me impatiently, and asked, "Where's the hammer?" (I groaned silently because I knew that his doing home repairs meant trouble and that, once again, I would be doing damage control at the hardware store.) "The hammer?" I repeated, "I think it's in the tool box." He looked at me with an incredulous expression on his face, as if I had just said something horribly nasty, and boomed, "*Judith, where's the hammer?*" I thought to myself, "I teach communication, so maybe he wants me to talk louder. *It's in the toolbox,*" I boomed back. Judging from his reaction, I was wrong.

Now, after we had finished "discussing" the whereabouts of the hammer loudly enough for all the neighbors to hear, I finally broke the code. "Where's the hammer?" really meant "Go get the hammer and bring it to me." All right, I thought, when it was all over and I had cooled down, I can learn how to do this. If the game is played this way, I'm ready for it.

Two weeks later, after a long day at the office for Wayne and a day of seminars and a horrible two-hour Los Angeles traffic jam for me, we ended up back in the kitchen. As we finished sorting the mail, Wayne looked at the clock and said, "No wonder I'm so hungry, it's 7:30." The code. I knew the code, and I was ready! Instead of saying, "Dinner? I've just been in two hours of traffic, I'm exhausted and you want me to make dinner?" My response was, "Oh, thank you for sharing that with me." As I went off to change my clothes, I casually turned back and asked him to make the same dinner for me that he planned to make for himself. (I later found out the menu was cheese and crackers).

Does this sound totally foreign to you? Are you looking forward to trying something like it, or thinking that you could never be so bold as to displease somebody and horrified at the way I handled it? If you're stuck because you're being concerned about displeasing somebody, even your difficult man, you need to look at what your concerns are and what you are fearing.

Difficult men don't necessarily have to like everything that you say or do. Remember, nondifficult (let's not call them "easy") men are usually very secure, self-confident, and competent. These men usually do treat women as equals and see them as allies rather than threats. This is not to say that they don't also see them as sex objects, but they are able to separate their reactions and channel their behavior appropriately. What makes it easy for a man to deal with a woman as an equal is usually more about the man than the woman, but we still have to do the best we can. When you become really good at dealing with difficult men, the difficult men in your life probably won't even know that they're being dealt with.

Difficult men don't have to like you or your behavior, but we'd be kidding ourselves if we didn't acknowledge that it certainly makes things easier when they do. So tomorrow, don't go out with a difficult-man alienation quota, but if you have to go for broke, do it.

Carol checked into a resort hotel in hot and humid weather. When she was shown to her room, she was horrified to find that it was dark and musty, full of mold and mildew. Just standing on the carpet for two minutes resulted in about eight flea bites on her feet and ankles. While making her way back to the check-in desk, she noticed several lovely rooms with marble floors and freshly painted walls. She complained to the male clerk about her room and requested one of the others. The clerk shook his head in a "there, there" way and smiled. It was impossible to change her room. She shook her head and smiled, too. Then, she leaned over the desk and countered, "I'm on vacation. I have nowhere to go and nothing to do, so I'll gladly stand here and wait until one becomes available." "You can't do that," the clerk objected. "You'll have to step aside. We have a lot of other people checking in today." "Oh, that's okay," she told him. "Since I'm not moving, you can just talk and work around me." And with that, she leaned even more comfortably on the desk, pulled out a novel, smiled up at him, and began to read. She had her new room within five minutes. Needless to say, she did not bond with the reception clerk, but she didn't have to. She was crossing this hotel off her list.

Now, what about your relationships at work? It really helps if people, at the least, don't mind being around you. Love you? Not important. Want to invite you home to dinner? Uh-uh. Retch or seethe at the thought of talking to you? Here, we have a problem.

Some women seem to carry an axe around with them and use it whenever they encounter the least bit of resistance. You know the type, and maybe you are the type. They squash an ant with a hammer. True, work is not a popularity contest, but there is such a thing as consistently coming on too strong. Remember, we don't want to destroy difficult men; we just want to change the relationships we have with them, and the next chapter will help us do just that.

Skills
for
Thriving

Some of the change-producing techniques in this chapter may be totally new to you, and some you may have used extensively, but never consciously, as tools for dealing with difficult men. As you read those ideas that are very different from what you're accustomed to, be aware of your own resistance, the "yes, buts" that you'll inevitably come up with. So many of us are afraid to change the status quo, to make the moves, to walk the walk and talk the talk that will assist us in getting to a new place. It is not easy to grow, and sometimes it is downright uncomfortable, but you should know that I'm on to you. I know that by resisting change, you're erecting your own barriers and helping the difficult-men in your life keep you right where they want you. Don't do it! Since you already know that you can change difficult-men's behavior by starting with your own, resolve to do it and move forward.

● LEARN TO USE A FOREIGN LANGUAGE: BODY LANGUAGE

Let's begin by focusing on body language, which for most of us is a foreign language that we can easily learn to speak, control, and use to our advantage.

One picture is worth a thousand words, and our body language provides volumes of information for difficult men to read and use against us. A shopping mall, an office, movies, theater lobby, bus, or any public place is a perfect spot for testing this idea. The next time you have a moment or two, take a good look around and check out women, keeping two things in mind. First, how are the women dressed? This is important, since this is the package that body language is wrapped in. Do they look serious, credible, appealing, seductive, professional, confident, easy on the eyes, flashy, babyish, cheap, or anything else? Whatever you decide is okay, and I don't suggest you go up to them and share your opinions, but don't stop there with these preliminary observations. Look again. How much of the image they project is the clothing they're wearing and how much is the way they carry themselves, their gestures, their posture, or the physical space they keep between them and any men they might be with? Now check them out one more time. If they are in conversations with men, what are they doing? Do they make direct eye contact? Are their arms folded; are their hands in their pockets, on their hips, on the man's hips (just kidding), where? All of these gestures are important since they give difficult men signals about what they can or cannot get away with.

So that you will learn enough about body language to do it justice, I'll give you a map to follow. The face is our first stop, since it is the area that can contain or give away the most. Brenda, a client of mine, fondly remembers when a tough male business associate with whom she had just clinched a deal remarked to her, "You know, when you smile, you look absolutely harmless; nobody can see the horns." She chuckles every time she repeats this remark, because she knows that working on using her smile has not taken that long but has continually brought great benefits in all areas of her life.

Joan, on the other hand, remembers her constant frustration when her difficult male boss, after telling her to do something used to say to her, "I know you don't want to do it, and this is just another example of your bad attitude." Joan's boss had read her facial expression and been able to see how she was feeling and apparently what she was thinking. This was not a good situation, since he ended up firing her before she had lined up a new job.

When choosing your facial expressions, pay attention to how you want to appear to each of your difficult men and then monitor their reactions and comments. Establish eye contact without squinting, glaring, or looking wide-eyed and overwhelmed. Smile, but not too broadly. Use a medium smile so that you look neither too controlled, nor too bubbly. Don't flare your nostrils. A lot of people have this habit without realizing it, and it's counterproductive for two reasons. The first is that it is not particularly pleasant to look up someone's nostrils (and as a short person, I tell you that you'd be amazed at what you see up there!). And the second is that it clearly shows your tension level, and that's nobody's business except yours, unless you decide to share it with them. (Of course, we don't care if difficult men do it, since it will give us more information about their anger and stress levels.)

And when it comes to lips, remember that licking or biting them, corners turned up, corners turned down, pursed tightly together—each of these gives a clear sign about what we are thinking and just exactly how we are feeling.

A lot more women than men blush. Blushing can be a real problem when you're with difficult men; it is like having a neon sign on your forehead flashing messages like "out of control," "panicked," "shy," "sexually attracted," and "uh-oh," to name a few. What can I tell you about blushing except that even if you are afflicted with it now, you will get over it as you develop your communication, confrontation, and positioning skills.

It goes without saying that everything I have just told you to be aware of on your own face is also exactly what you need to look for when talking to or observing the face of a difficult man. Put all the facial clues into some kind of perspective, however; don't just take one observation and isolate it. For example, a difficult man licking his lips can mean lust, nervousness, or preparation to pounce (verbally, not physically). It can also mean leftover crumbs from lunch, though, so watch it.

Chris, the six-foot-tall, very strong, and very blond

person we talked about before, uses her smile to disarm difficult men in business transactions, because they make the mistake of thinking they can take advantage of the fact that she's a woman. When she wants the advantage, she smiles a lot and tilts her head, which is very confusing to them because they get mixed messages. Is she a very assertive woman or the stereotypical dumb blonde? Her response to this? She says to herself, "You think I'm a dumb blonde? Right, good, keep thinking that." She laughs at the concept of dumb blondes because she finally figured out that the word *dumb* really should be applied to the behavior of the men who deal with blondes, not to the blondes themselves. A refreshing attitude from a very secure, very tall woman who could have all sorts of complexes from growing up in a society that says that girls (and women) are supposed to be shorter, weaker, and more petite than boys (and men).

There are a few other female body-language faux pas exhibited by the women I see every day in my work and my personal life. Aside from rounded shoulders, no-neck tortoise posture, and busts as headlights, here are the worst ones, the ones that give difficult men the upper hand in about a one-and-a-half seconds:

The limp wrist. You've seen it. The arm is bent in a right angle, the elbow is against the body between the bust and the waist, and the fingers are pointing down. The arm looks as if it's in a sling, but there is no sling.

The pigeon-toed position. Men look at this one and see, "Attack me (verbally), because I am an easy target. I'll probably just fall over, because my knees will knock and throw me off balance." Plus, pigeon toes for some reason seem to accompany fidgeting fingers, a dead give-away for nervousness.

The breast-protector look. This one, with the arms folded over or under the bust, is particularly interesting. On women with large breasts, it looks as if their arms are sitting on or under a shelf. The message, when accompanied by a scowl, is often "Don't even think of coming near me." If accompanied by a weak smile or the head tilted to one side, it is "I'm scared, and I'm protecting myself from you because I know that you are stronger than I am."

The bird-head look. This is the one where women tilt their heads to one side, thus making themselves look a lot like sparrows listening and waiting for who-knows-what. Call me crazy, but I don't associate sparrows with strength or the notion of forces to be reckoned with, and neither do difficult men.

The hands-on-hips position. This usually transmits the message "I am ticked, and if I take my hands off my hips, I'll probably wrap them around your throat." It immediately gives away the fact that someone has gotten to you and made you angry. Not good.

Sitting or standing with legs apart. The statement behind this stance may be "I was a trucker in a former life" or "Come on, big boy" or "Window shopping, any-one?" When women do this wearing pants, it's not great but not terrible, either; in a skirt, it can be a real problem.

Firing with the trigger finger. This maneuver—

pointing at the other person with your index finger, usually aiming at their face or chest—is accusatory and attacking and usually results in a defensive response.

There are many other poses that we could talk about, but you get the idea. Be aware of your body language to make sure that you're saying what you want the difficult man to hear and not a thing more.

Turnabout is fair play, however, so watch body language very closely to get whatever clues you can. With difficult men, there are a few specific body parts to watch for. Just as a woman's all-over posture, when extreme, tends to go one of two ways, men also tend to display just a few extreme behaviors.

One of these behaviors is the pelvic thrust, often exhibited by middle-aged males in midlife crisis who also may use hair spray on their chests, which we are unfortunate enough to see when they leave their shirts unbuttoned all the way down to their bellybuttons. When you see the pelvic thrust and/or hair-sprayed chest, it means you are getting a huge testosterone alert. These guys interpret almost everything a woman does as a signal that she is sexually attracted to them. Therefore, when a woman says to one of these guys, "I like your Porsche," he hears, "You look like a hard-driving stud, take me *now*." Okay, maybe I'm exaggerating a little, but you know the type. So, be careful about your body language when you talk to them. I also find that wearing sensible shoes, support hose, a Cross-Your-Heart bra, and a few strategically placed dabs of Clearasil helps lessen their intensity.

Another common exhibition of male body language

is the more aggressive stance, which often includes finger pointing, sharp hand and arm movements, or leaning forward on both hands across the desk or table. A steely glare, very serious frown, or eye rolling are also big power moves. Don't be intimidated or put off by any of these. Watch it when it is happening, and say to yourself, "Hmmm, I read about this in my DWDM book." Distance yourself emotionally.

There are also those body-language moves that some men still use at work today because they refuse to acknowledge the sexual harassment rules and regulations. We all know the "I'm just a hugging kind of guy" or the guy who has decided that he's the official office neck and back massager for all the women he can get his hands on. This male body language—touching a woman without her permission and assuming that she likes it—demonstrates the difficult-man tendency to invade a woman's space. When a difficult man travels into your space without a passport, get ready to move or to use your own facial expression to stake out your territory. Don't say anything nasty. You can even make a joke of it to lighten the tension and say, "Wait a second, Joe, when you sit or stand so close, my eyes cross and I can't see you."

Let's say you do feel tense when you are talking to a difficult male. Since you don't want to let him see how you feel, you know for certain that biting your nails or gnawing on your fists is not recommended. Biting his nails or gnawing on his fists is also definitely not recommended. The best hand gesture is the steeple position— hands in front of you with all ten fingertips touching, forming a V. Doing this, you can push your fingers together to do something with the tension. If you are sitting, make sure that you keep the small of your back pressed against the back of your chair to prevent you from leaning or lunging forward, since this would show your intense reaction and desire to push your point. Don't recline way back, which would demonstrate your desire to get away from him because he has succeeded in making you feel vulnerable.

I see women in meetings with difficult men undermine themselves constantly because they've only learned how to put on a happy face and friendly demeanor instead of wearing a poker face and a neutrally positioned body.

Many years ago, as a fairly new sexuality instructor presenting a course to a group of several hundred policemen, I made the mistake of wearing just a skirt with a silky blouse. It was very cold in the room, and I was nervous. Ten minutes into my talk, I noticed that no one in the room was looking at my face. When I realized why, it became apparent that to scrape together any shred of dignity, I had to keep one arm across my bust and write and point to the charts I was using with the other. I looked anything but in control. Needless to say, ever since that time I have gone to no presentations without a jacket. Make sure that you are prepared for whatever you might have to deal with in the body-language department.

Pete, the husband of a friend of mine, gleefully (until she poked him) recalled, "I remember years ago when women used to wear miniskirts and men used to throw dimes on the office floor to get the women to bend over to pick them up." I am not sure what makes me more upset, the fact that men did something like this or that they only used dimes. It is sad to also realize that even today in a power-loaded position at work a lot of men would still throw dimes and a lot of women would still bend over.

We still have a lot of changes to make. Begin by packaging yourself effectively, taking advantage of your control over your body language and using your ability to read the body language of any difficult men you might encounter.

● LISTEN TO WHAT THEY'RE SAYING AND TO WHAT THEY'RE NOT

Tuning up your listening skills is not unlike encasing yourself in a bulletproof glass bubble. It's as if you are surrounding yourself in a safe environment: "I can hear you, I can see you, and I can engage with you, but you can't hurt me, because I alone have the key to open this bubble. I can choose to make myself vulnerable with direct contact whenever I want, but I can also choose to protect myself."

Gerda, a very effective consultant who works with difficult men all the time, enjoys listening. It provides her the opportunity to "let the train run on by" when she knows that nothing she can say will make them really stop and listen. "I can get hit by the train if I step in front of it, so instead, I step aside, watch it pass, and then decide my next move."

Chris puts it a little differently: "I listen; it's as if I'm lying in wait. Like a battleship. I know my time will come." She's right, too!

Sometimes, when you really listen to what a difficult man is saying, you hear amazing things, and you discover why you've gotten trapped so often in the past. You realize that what you are hearing when he asks an apparently innocent question is really what many people refer to as QWAP, "questions with answers provided." These are not really questions, and there are no right answers except his. That's why you can never win in these situations. Becoming aware of this will help you avoid needless angry and dead-end discussions. Some examples might be:

"Don't you think it's too late to eat?"

"You aren't going to wear that, are you?"

"You don't really think it will work, do you?"

Just how important is listening? Sara wanted to sell her handcrafted jewelry and contacted a department-store buyer who was approached by hundreds of people a year. Before the meeting, she added up all her costs, which totaled $40 per piece of jewelry. She was nervous because she thought she would be asking too much and pricing herself out of the market. When she finally had her face-to-face meeting with the buyer, he breezed in twenty minutes late, looked at his watch, sat down, showed his difficult-man boredom with a sneering "I'm too busy to give you a lot of my time" look, and before she could get a word out, immediately took over the meeting and began telling her about all the problems he'd have with her necklaces, specifically the packaging they'd have to do and the display challenges they'd face. As she was listening to him, she began thinking about how she could reduce her costs. She was getting entirely too wrapped up in her own thoughts, but luckily, she allowed herself to tune back into him and what he was saying. She was shaking inside when all of sudden the buyer said, "So, in light of all this, I'd only be able to offer you $75 apiece." She almost fell off her chair.

Listening is a very powerful DMN (difficult-man neutralizer); when done well, it can really give you an edge.

Here is an opportunity to take stock of your listening habits. Grade yourself on the following behaviors, keeping in mind what happens to you when a difficult man begins doing his difficult thing. This is not about how you listen to a friend or someone with whom you have a great open and equal relationship. It is about what happens to your listening habits in an emotionally charged, testosterone-based encounter.

For each of the following behaviors, grade yourself according to this scale:

A = Always

B = Almost always

C = Rarely

D = Never

1. I allow the difficult man to finish his sentence and/or complete thought before I begin to respond.

2. I listen to what the difficult man really means, whether or not his words are actually saying it.

3. I make myself stay focused on what the difficult man is saying, even if I am repulsed by him for something he has already done or because he reminds me of another undesirable difficult man.

4. I ignore distractions and tune out everything around me and listen only to the difficult man.

5. I look and sound as if I am interested in and considering that which the difficult man is saying.

How did you do? The more A's the better.

Let's take a look at each of these techniques and discuss why they are so effective.

Number 1: Not cutting the difficult man off too soon is important for several reasons, the main one being that you won't get all the information he might be willing to give you. Sara is a good example of this. The other reason is that you already know what you have to say, and you need to take the time to really hear what the DM has to say.

If you are an extrovert, or an "outie," as we will discuss later on, you probably need to pay particular attention to this technique, and if you do cut him off, a good comeback would be "Excuse me, I got so interested in what you were saying that I jumped ahead of myself." Then really listen by making yourself count to ten (to yourself) between the time the DM closes his mouth and you open yours.

Number 2: Listening between the lines is something we've discussed before. For example, when your DM boss says, "I'm not sure your idea would work," he often means something like "If I say yes to you, Joe and Fred will be upset, and I don't want to deal with that." You have to be willing to check out what you think the DM might mean and pay particular attention to whether or not he is really saying no.

Number 3: Try to get beyond your reactions of anger, dislike, or disgust. Listen to each DM and regard what he's saying as a brand-new opportunity to gather the information you need, not as a time to "once again be subjected to garbage I can't use and don't want to ever hear again."

Number 4: Ignoring distractions is a matter of focusing. The more you listen, the more the DM gives, and the more he gives, the better you've got it. Here is your opportunity to practice your creative and controlled use of facial expressions. Show interest with eye contact and body language. Look relaxed and appear interested by not falling asleep or striking an on-guard position.

Number 5: Showing interest has to do with faking it. You have to work hard to find some shred of information to keep your interest, even if it is only your amazement at what he is saying or trying to do. It sometimes helps if you think of yourself as an anthropologist, listening intently to understand this interesting specimen.

What is the upshot of all this? Go back and look at your responses to all these items. The more you practice these five listening habits, the better a listener you will be. You do have to think before you open your mouth, and the only true way to think accurately is to listen to what the DM is saying, implying, or not saying by holding back.

When your emotions are revved up, your perceptions are skewed. You say things that you mean, you just don't mean to say them. You disclose information you would not normally disclose if you were calm. If you work on listening more and speaking impulsively less, you won't have as many disclosure regrets.

There is a time to speak up and a time to clam up. When you decide to clam up, also decide to listen up. Punctuate your listening with affirming techniques that will appeal to the egos of difficult men. Throw in the occasional, "Uh-huh," "I see," or the Johnny Carson special, "I didn't know that." Difficult men love this stuff.

With three magic words, "Isn't that interesting," you can get them to give you more information than you ever imagined. Nod, smile if appropriate to express pleasure, and maintain eye contact. Repeat in your own words some of what they've said ("So you think that I have been spending too much time with my friends") and listen to them excitedly say, "Yes, because," and then spill the beans about what's really bothering them.

Listening is one part of communicating and dealing effectively with difficult men. Another is talking. A critical step is questioning, the way you ask for information.

● GET THE INFORMATION YOU NEED WITHOUT GETTING THEIR GOAT

If you listen really well when difficult men talk, you'll have the opportunity to ask the crucial questions. Please note that "Are you crazy?" or "You're kidding, aren't you?" or "How long have you been delusionary?" aren't the kinds of questions I have in mind.

To prepare yourself, read the following questions and answer them without thinking too much.

1. How old are you?

2. What are some of your fondest vacation memories?

3. How hard is it for you to get up in the morning?

4. What kinds of things do you do best?

5. What time does your work day end?

Questions 1 and 5 are closed questions. They get answers that are focused and specific. You probably said a number (or maybe "None of your business") to number 1 and a number or "Not soon enough" to number 5. Questions 2, 3, and 4 are open questions. You probably thought more about these and began to recall more information in response to them. This is because open questions make it easier for you to give a lot of information by eliminating boundaries, while closed questions usually do not promote a dialogue.

Watch how open and closed questions can help you start conversations on your terms or focus on getting what you need.

> BOSS: *Charlene, you have a bad attitude; no, actually you have a lousy attitude.*
>
> CHARLENE: *Please describe what I did that you didn't like. (Open)*
>
> BOSS: *You were very rude to that customer.*
>
> CHARLENE: *What exactly are you referring to? (Closed)*
>
> BOSS: *You refused to go out with him.*

Charlene now has enough information to know that she is not willing to meet her boss's expectations. She can now ask another closed question.

> CHARLENE: *Is that one of your requirements for this job?*

Depending on his answer, she can decide what to do next.

Charlene used a combination of open and closed questions to get all the facts she needed. In this case, she can introduce the subject of sexual harassment or she can tell him that going out with a customer is not part of her job description.

Just asking these questions, however, is not enough if you want to be successful. Just as we erode our credibility with our body language, we women unknowingly undermine and negate our own questions by inserting minimizing words or prefacing them with modifiers.

Do these patterns sound familiar?

"I just want to ask..."

"I'm only asking if..."

"This is probably a stupid question, but..."

"I was just wondering if..."

"Is it okay if I ask a question..."

"Would you mind if I..."

"Are you sure that I can..."

"Maybe if I..."

"I'm probably the only one who doesn't know this, but..." .

No, no, no! Just writing these examples makes me cringe, because it reminds me of how we belittle ourselves before difficult men even try to do it to us.

As if it's not enough that we cloud our questions with words that make us sound weak and unsure, we then compound the problem with our tone of voice and inflection. Have you ever noticed how women's voices often take on a flirtatious or insecure quality, particularly when we soften our voices and end sentences with an "up" tone or a giggle? Stop and think of all the messages we can send just by asking one question.

So, do be careful when you are asking questions. Make sure that your voice, your body language, and the content of your questions are all going in the same direction and sending the message you want your DM to receive. Questions asked effectively will not elicit defensive or aggressive responses. Directness or persistence, that's what you're aiming for.

● POLITICALLY CORRECT CONFRONTING

Confronting difficult men without alienating or angering them is an art. When done well, it is truly a thing of beauty, and when not done well, the details are too gory to recount. If you are not willing to confront, it is probably because you've never learned how to do it, or you've never seen it done well. When I ask even the most senior executives I coach, who are usually men, which they would rather do, chew a piece of ice with a tooth that needs a root canal or confront someone face-to-face, 99.9 percent of the time they say, "Pass the ice."

Confrontation is a learned skill, and the good news is that it doesn't take long to become skilled at using it. It is really a feedback tool, designed to organize information so that the person getting the feedback or being confronted can hear it easily and if possible, painlessly.

To help you position yourself so that you can confront logically and intellectually instead of emotionally and frantically, I am going to give you a foolproof recipe that has actually changed the lives of a lot of the women (and men) I work with, individually or in groups. This technique is not lengthy or complicated, and when used properly, it doesn't even seem like a technique, because it really is just a matter-of-fact way of organizing information.

To confront a DM—or any person, for that matter—organize what you want to say in five steps:

1. **Give your perspective of the situation**, as if you've taken a picture or a sound recording of his speech or behavior. The words to use are:

   "When you..."

   This is also a model for giving feedback—your observation of what your difficult man is doing or has done in a way that is descriptive and specific.

2. **Give your understanding**, of what he's said or done.

   "I understand this to mean..."

3. **Describe what impact** this had on you.

   "As a result, I..." or

   "This is (was) important because..."

4. Describe your gut reaction.

"I feel..."

Notice the absence of the word "that" in this step, since "that" turns this into an opinion (step 2) and not a feeling. Feelings are pure: happy, sad, scared, intimidated, overwhelmed, elated, anxious, delighted. This step is optional. Use it if you think it will add something, and leave it out if you think it will detract from the rest of the discussion.

5. State what you want regarding the situation.

"I want to..."

"My next step is to..."

"I intend to..."

Here is an example:

Your boss tells you that you are lazy, and you say to him, "*When you said to me*, 'You are lazy,' *I understood this to mean that* I had not done something you wanted me to do. *This is important to me because* I like this job, and I want to do it well. *I feel* concerned, and *I want to ask you to* tell me exactly what I didn't do and what you would like me to do now."

Quick, neat, and to the point. Here is another one:

Your Significant Other tells you that you don't care about what he wants. You say, "*When you said to me*, 'You don't care about what I want,' and you then slammed the door, *I understood it to mean that* you were angry at me and disappointed about my not doing something. *This is important to me because* I want to try to do what works for both of us. *I feel* hopeful that you and I can work this out. *I want you to* tell me exactly what I did that gave you the idea I don't care about what you want."

Let's look at how you might confront an unpleasant reaction from a difficult male coworker:

"When I stopped at your desk and asked for your part of the written report that we are supposed to be working on together, *you said to me,* 'I'll get it to you when I'm good and ready.' *I understood this to mean* that you are not concerned about the deadline I have to meet to complete my part of it. *This is important to me because* we will both be held accountable for the quality and completion of the report. *I feel* angry at you for your lack of consideration and team work. *I intend to* try to understand exactly what you are doing and go to our supervisor if you make it impossible for me to fulfill my responsibilities."

And here's how you might confront a doctor who you believe is discounting you and whatever is wrong with you: "*You said* that my pain is all in my head and that I should take tranquilizers to help me calm down. *I understand this to mean* you are not willing to take the time to find out more about what may be causing the pain.

"*This is important to me because* it is my health and well-being at risk. *I feel* angry at you and disappointed, and *I intend to* get a second opinion."

Sharp like a razor. Clear and direct. Now, you try one. Think of something that you want to confront.

Notice that I said something, not someone. Think about confronting the behavior or the issues, not the person. State it as succinctly as possible and then fill in the blanks. The biggest mistake that people make when doing this is to put step 2 material, interpretations, in the step 1 slot. Remember, to keep step 1 pure, think back to *Dragnet* ("Just the facts, ma'am") or Mr. Spock on *Star Trek*—unemotional detail.

Here are some other phrases that are handy for confronting:

When a DM implies a threat, but cloaks it ("I don't want to have to do something you might regret") respond, "That sounded like a threat. Is that what you intended?"

If a DM says, "A person like you is always causing trouble," ask, "How are you expecting me to interpret that remark?"

To a DM who says, "Your behavior surprises me," counter with, "What exactly are you trying to tell me?"

When a DM loses his cool and you want to find out why, inquire of him, "If you had spoken instead of pounding the table, what would you have said?"

When your DM boss shortchanges you on your raise, ask, "How does the raise you are giving me relate to my performance?"

For the difficult man who says, "You know my answer, don't even bother to ask," follow up with, "What exactly are you saying no to?" Or: "Perhaps I wasn't clear. Please indulge me. In your own words, what did you hear me asking you to do?" Or: "What would it take to get a positive response from you?"

When you confront, you must be prepared to hear the answer your difficult man gives you. It may not be what you want to hear, and that probably makes it even more important. Unless you lay out exactly what you know the person is doing or saying and hold it up so that it is viewed the same way by both of you or all concerned, you will get suckered into an emotional spiral that will either deteriorate rapidly or accelerate to an attacking exchange. What you don't know can hurt you, and what you do know you can work on fixing and changing.

Once you tell the other person that what he is doing bothers you, give your understanding of the situation, explain the reason that it is important to you, add your emotional response (or not), and articulate your plans, wants, or needs, you are giving feedback and confronting clearly. You can even go a step further and ask the difficult man for his reactions, ideas, or commitment to work on the problem.

Some possible follow-up questions are:

"What is your reaction to what I've just said?"

"Is there anything I've missed? If so, please fill in the blanks."

"Are you willing to work on resolving this with me?".

If he says, "Yes, I am willing to work it out," great! If the answer is no, you now know that you have a different issue to address.

Another method of confronting is to use contrasting

statements. You begin with what you expected, wanted, needed, or understood would happen and then contrast this with what you got or what actually did happen. It is important to be very specific when you do this.

Here are some examples:

"You told me that you would arrive by 6:00. You arrived at 8:30."

"You said that my raise would be seven percent. The raise you are saying I am getting is three percent."

"You assured me that you would pay off the credit-card bill by January 15. It is March 3, and there is still a balance of $800."

"I have told you eight times that my name is Judith. This is the ninth time that you have called me Muffy."

"Last week, I asked you to tell me in private when you are displeased with something I've done. This morning you yelled at me in front of my coworkers."

The pattern is always the same. It is very specific, very factual, and very unemotional. Everything is divided into expectations or commitments and results.

If you want to become proficient in using these confrontation techniques, you need to practice. My own method is to talk to the steering wheel in my car, which I find is a good start, since it doesn't talk back or laugh. Then I make my friends listen to what I have to say and how I plan to say it, and then coach me.

Don't think of yourself as imposing on your friends when you do this. In fact, it will be just the opposite.

You'll be coaching and helping them get ready to deal with their own difficult men. Make a day of it or at least a lunch.

● PUTTING IT ALL TOGETHER: PROBLEM SOLVING

Throughout this book, we have acknowledged that when you and a difficult man disagree, or when he does something you don't like, want, or need, you have a problem; the behavior is his, but, alas, the problem is yours.

You can address each problem in such a way as to take it to its natural completion, and not go over and over the same issues because you get tangled up and confused with heavy emotionalism. When you are angry or hurt, your thinking is not as clear as when you are calm, rational, focused, and relaxed. To compensate for this blip in your program, you need a systematic plan for streamlined problem solving. Here it is, six simple steps that will help you begin at the beginning, end at the end, and not take any unwanted, unplanned for, or unnecessary side trips.

Step 1: Make sure you and your difficult man agree on exactly what the problem or the main issue is. To do this, use your listening, questioning, and confronting skills. If you can't reach consensus on this, you will never reach consensus on a solution.

You can use your second confronting technique here:

"This is what you said that you would do, and it didn't happen. To me, what's important is to find out what can be done now to fix the situation."

Then ask:

"What do you see as the problem or main issue?"

Use your listening and clarifying skills here.

"Let me see if I understand. Are you saying that...?"

Once you have agreement, go to step 2.

Step 2: State your desire to work on the problem or issue and ask your difficult man if he is willing to do the same.

If he says yes, proceed to step 3. If he says no, go back to your questioning skills and find out why.

"You say you are unwilling to work on solving this problem. Help me understand the reasons."

If your difficult man tells you that he doesn't want to talk about it, deal with it, or hear about it again, and you see neon lights flashing above his head that read, "Get used to it," you have to decide what you want to do next. Two options immediately come to mind. The first is to write him off and work around him. The second is to give him some reasons to get him to take another look at his decision.

Step 3: If he sees the light, move to this step: Each of you take a turn to describe what happened, how you got to this point, and what your choices are for solving the problem. Come up with as many possibilities as you can.

> *"What are all the different ways this problem could be resolved?"*

Don't discard any ideas. Sometimes the best solutions come as a result of the most unusual suggestion. So make sure that you lay the ground rules, one of which is that it's not okay to say things like "that won't work," until you can test all the ideas for feasibility.

Step 4: Step 4 is just that, testing for feasibility, seeing which possible solution might fly.

> *"Let's look at the advantages and disadvantages of each idea and then choose the one that we agree to be the best."*

It is sometimes helpful to acknowledge your difficult man's feelings or what you think are his feelings.

> *"I know this is important to you. It is to me, too. That's why it's hard for me to do what we're doing now, asking you to join me in looking at something different."*

And at times, you may find it helpful to slip in a pre-condition:

> *"I'd be willing to go to your parent's house for Christmas after you come to mine for Thanksgiving."*

The forced-choice technique that uses a closed question isn't really a great example of diplomacy, but it does deserve some mention since it gets to the heart of the issue:

> *"Which would you prefer, going to visit my family for Thanksgiving or going to visit your family for Christmas alone?"*

Step 5: Choose the solution that sounds best and plan how to make it happen.

> *"Okay, who will do what, by when, and how will we know that everything is okay?"*

This step introduces accountability, which is critical if you want to sustain long-lasting positive results. This is where the rubber meets the road, and your difficult man moves from talk to action.

Step 6: This is the "so-what" learning step, where you can acknowledge the positive outcome and plan for the next time there is a problem to work through.

> *"This really worked well. What can you and I do differently next time to take advantage of what we've accomplished?"*

Now you have it, a no-frills problem-solving approach that is painless and effective. It combines a few of your new skills and can help get you through the murkiest of situations.

Adjusting your attitude was your first step in dealing with difficult men. These new skills will be another important part of the dealing-with-difficult-men equation. The third part is the matter of positioning and strategy; this is where you'll learn how to be conflict savvy: what to do when and when to do what.

```
C   H   A   P   T   E   R
```

5

Conflict
Savvy

Many women, once they've gained some new skills
and insight, view the difficult men in their lives as fresh
meat, and as a result, they make the mistake of indis-
criminately trying to apply everything they've learned
all at once and right away. Since difficult men are not
all alike and the situations they create are often complex
and multidimensional as well, I don't recommend this.
To be effective at stopping them dead in their tracks, we
have to be selective about what to do, how we do it,
and, most important, when we do it. Positioning is
everything.

When women try to confront or out-think the difficult men in their lives without adequate preparation and
forethought, they often inadvertently escalate the exist-
ing conflict and cause even more problems. Because I
want you to experience success and not fall into this

trap, my goal in this chapter is to help you become conflict savvy.

● THE LAST CHECK-IN POINT

But, before you decide what to do when and when to do what, you have to decide whether to do it at all. So, before you get even more fired up, answer these questions about your difficult man:

1. Have you decided that his behavior is truly unacceptable? ....YES NO

2. Do you feel anxious every time you know you are going to see him?................YES NO

3. Do you react negatively when you're with him? ....YES NO

4. Do you find yourself actually waiting for him to be difficult?..........................YES NO

5. Is a relationship with him important to you for social, emotional, or political reasons?..YES NO

6. Do you feel worse about yourself after you've spent time with him than you did before?.............................YES NO

7. Do you want to change the way he treats you?...YES NO

8. If you never saw him again, would it
matter to you?..YES   NO

9. Does his behavior affect the way
other people see or treat you?......................YES   NO

10. If and when you've said something
to him in the past, has he turned it
around and used it against you?.................YES   NO

If you answered no to number 5, 8, or 9, I strongly suggest that you reconsider whether you should deal with him or just remove him from your life or you from his life altogether. If you answered yes to the other questions, you have indicated that you care enough. Now you have to investigate just how much both of you care and what both of your emotional investments will mean regarding what you do.

As I've said before, like it or not, our emotions get involved in our dealings with difficult men. When we have a strong emotional investment, we have more at stake, so the decisions we make and the actions we take are much more important than they would be if we really didn't care very much at all. The same is true for each of the difficult men we deal with. The higher the stakes, the tougher the resistance they will put up, because they care more. You can use information about the degree of emotional investment you and your difficult man have to determine whether or not the time is right to deal with an issue; decide how you should position yourself, and assess whether or not the issue itself is important enough to be dealt with at all.

Look at the following diagram. It has four squares: two pertain to your emotional investment, and two concern your difficult man's emotional investment. The four combinations each suggest a different plan of action.

The Emotional Investment Assessment

	I care	I don't care
He cares	Not negotiable to me **①** Not negotiable to him	Negotiable to me **②** Not negotiable to him
He doesn't care	Not negotiable to me **③** Negotiable to him	Negotiable to me **④** Negotiable to him

The best way to use these squares is to look at each of the combinations and decide which is most like the emotional-investment combination shared by you and your difficult man regarding one of your problem issues. Based on your diagnosis, what, if any, steps would you take?

If square 1 describes your situation, you need to proceed slowly and cautiously. Since both of you have strong emotional investments, neither of you will willingly back off. Do your homework. Decide what motivates your difficult man (chapter 2) and figure out a strategy to provide some of what he needs. Use questions to find out what's behind his emotional investment and use listening skills (chapter 4) to hear any hidden meanings or information.

If square 2 describes your emotional-investment combination, you are in particularly good shape, because you have some unencumbered alternatives. Regardless of the type of difficult man you are dealing with, since you don't care much about the issue, you can take whatever action you want or score points by being giving. You also can decide to go after what you want and not be flexible. It depends upon your past experiences with this man and what you're trying to accomplish. Use your feedback or step 1 of your confronting skills, feedbacking what you think he wants and why it's important to him (chapter 4) to let him know how tuned in you are to his issue.

If square 3 is where you fit, you have to be a little more cautious. Since he doesn't have a big emotional investment and you do (just the reverse of square 2), in this case, he is on easy street. Just because he doesn't care doesn't necessarily mean that he wants to share. You still need to position yourself so that you don't appear too anxious or vulnerable. Borrow some of the Logic Pusher's tactics (chapter 2), and prepare yourself with unemotional facts. It can't hurt to also know what category your difficult man falls into (chapter 2) so that you can make your pitch or react to his in a way to which he will respond to best.

Finally, we come to square 4, where the issue, emotional-investmentwise, is no big whoopie to either of you. This is a good place to be, because everything is up for grabs (except you, of course). Still, don't let down your guard too much; your difficult man might realize something along the way and change his mind and his degree of caring, so prepare for it. Don't let something go without enough thought to ensure that even if he did change his mind, the outcome would still be okay with you. In this case, ask yourself open questions (chapter 4) to really think it through. Don't give something away because you think that neither you and your difficult man care about it, if, upon finding out that he had changed his mind and did care, you would be upset.

Use this information to help you decide what to do when and when to do what. By assessing who cares and who doesn't and where both of you are, you can make a better choice regarding what, when, and how to act. Don't let the fact that you care erode your effectiveness.

● WHEN TO SPEAK UP, WHEN TO CLAM UP

Knowing *when* and *if* to confront your difficult man is almost as important as knowing how. There are certain situations that are appropriate and others that aren't.

Speak up when:

1. You stand to gain more than you lose.

2. It's your job to say something.

3. You want to create a work environment that reflects mutual respect.

4. You want honesty without hostility.

5. You don't want to condone future behavior.

6. You need to take care of your own interests.

7. You are not trying to teach him a lesson.

8. You are not preoccupied with flexing your own power.

9. You know the system will support your action.

10. You are not trying to make him look bad in order to make yourself look good.

11. You want to feel good about yourself and your behavior.

12. You have already unloaded and vented your anger far away from him, and now you are ready to talk about it.

A basic rule of thumb when deciding whether or not to take on a difficult man is: If it makes a difference to you, go for it. If it doesn't, don't. Life is too short to sweat the small stuff. I often ask myself, "How will I feel tomorrow if I deal with the difficult man, and how will I feel tomorrow if I don't?" If it won't make a difference in my tomorrow, I clam up. If it will, I speak up.

Let's start with a basic question: Is your difficult man an Innie or an Outie (not as in belly button but as in personality); that is, is he quiet or does he talk? And why does this matter?

Whether your difficult man is motivated by his need for power, admiration, or nurturing, dealing with him effectively means gearing your communication to his Innie- or Outie-ness.

The Innie, it must be said, doesn't necessarily keep quiet to make you crazy, although sometimes it is his way of dealing with anger and displeasure. He often holds back in order to blame you later for what you did or didn't do according to what he did or didn't want. Don't compensate for his silence and withholding. In other words, don't keep talking for the sake of trying to force him to speak up. Acknowledge his silence. "I just asked you a question, and you didn't answer. I don't know how to interpret that." Or you could say, "If you had just answered my question out loud the way you undoubtedly did silently to yourself, what would I have heard you say?" These questions are not hostile; they are probing. See the section in chapter 4 on open questions. Just make sure that you don't have a dagger on the end of your probe.

If you are an Innie and your difficult man is also an Innie, the one thing we don't have to worry about is one of you cutting the other one off in midsentence. In fact, we probably should be concerned about both of you using complete sentences. Okay, I'm exaggerating. But two Innies are really not very likely to get issues out on the table unless things get pretty revved up. It's not that they don't feel, it's just that they don't tend to talk about how they feel. If you are an Innie, you can choose to keep your mouth shut or to open it, but when you don't open it, know that the other person can continue to act however he desires. Open your mouth when the time is right for you, not for him.

An Outie is a very different animal. Not only does he talk, but he believes that people actually want and need to hear what he has to say. He exudes, he expresses, he expands, he spews, he usually outtalks you and cuts you off in midsentence. You have to be quick to get a word in edgewise with an Outie. He doesn't hold back very well, and listening isn't often his strong suit. So, if you're an Innie dealing with an Outie, take advantage of the fact that you listen better than he does and be prepared to use what you hear (chapter 4). Outies do listen for one thing: their name. They always hear it, so when you want to get their attention, start by saying their name. Don't embellish it; instead of "Ron, you jerk," just "Ron" will do. Sprinkle his name liberally throughout your comments, but be careful not to overdo. When dealing with an Outie, make sure to give him a structure that will enable you to control what you say and at the same time force him to listen.

> *"Ron, I really am interested in what you just said, and I want to add two main points to your ideas. The first is ... and the second is ..."*

You've just gotten the Outie to close his mouth, and

you've reserved his brain for two points' worth of time. If you really want to excel, hold your hand in front of you, palm up, and raise two fingers counting off your points as you make them. This gives the Outie some visual cues as well. I am not being sarcastic here. Visual cues help the Outie to focus. Just make sure that your tone of voice is not sarcastic.

If you are an Outie and your difficult man is an Innie, you've got some work in the self-control department to do. As an Outie, you probably tend to try to take over whether you mean to or not, and this is not good. If you do all the talking, your Innie can just sit back and do nothing, and all you know is what you've said. There is still a very important part of the equation that has had no input. You may also be giving the Innie validation for not participating, providing the resistance he needs to keep his distance. So ask your question and close your mouth. Be prepared to wait in silence for an answer. If you don't get one, ask again.

Darlene, a definite Outie, was on a road trip with a Self-Proclaimed Expert who was also an Outie. This means that both of them were outgoing, strong, and probably pretty pushy. At a certain point, Darlene knew exactly which freeway to take to get to their destination and so did he, or so he thought. He snapped at her when she said, "I think we should go north." As soon as she saw his reaction, she decided that it just wasn't worth it to argue. They were going to a function given by his friends and if they were late, it would be his problem. She put aside her Outie behavior, settled back in her seat, and waited for him to find out the hard way, which he did after driving twenty miles in the wrong direction.

On a subsequent trip, as soon as she knew he was about to go the wrong way, she pulled out a map and said, "Would you like to check your route?" He looked at her, checked the map, and took the correct route. She didn't give him even one "I told you so." She had made her point, allowed him to come out looking good, and had avoided another forty-minute detour. It can be just that simple if you know whom and what you're dealing with, you prepare in advance, and you are willing to change your style to fit the situation.

● HOW TO MAKE IT BETTER

In every encounter we have with difficult men, until we become aware of our own behavior as well as what really makes them tick, we can hardly help making certain mistakes. These mistakes, resulting in the escalation of conflict, intensify the difficult man's feelings of anger and resistance to what we are trying to do. Often, women forget some simple conflict de-escalation techniques.

A few tactics are particularly effective at de-escalating conflict. Keep these in mind and use them in combination with the other skills and techniques you are learning about.

Try, when appropriate, to:

1. **Use humor.** This is tricky, because although laughter can be the best medicine, it can also be inappropriate and offensive. Acknowledge your gut but listen to your head on this one.

2. **Find common ground.** Point out similarities instead of differences. We will talk more about this one in the section on conflict routes coming up next.

3. **Show willingness and flexibility.** Don't come in with a chair and a whip (showing). You can always back up, and you will do better with flexibility.

4. **Focus on one issue at a time.** That's all anybody, difficult men or regular people, can do.

5. **Be as factual as you can.** Unless you have decided that this is a good time to try an emotional appeal, stick to a few solid facts and keep away from the fluff.

6. **Show respect and empathy for the difficult man's position.** Difficult men respond well to this approach, and it makes you look (and feel) really good!

Even when you feel yourself losing control or you change your mind about your desired level of participation in a given situation, you can always de-escalate the conflict if you:

1. **Keep your tone of voice consistent.** Sound as natural as you can. If anything, lower your tone. Don't raise it (chapter 4).

2. **Keep sarcasm for one-shot deals only.** Difficult men forgive, but they don't forget. The aftereffects of sarcasm will come back to haunt you in a long-term relationship, and the conflict shouldn't be about winning. It should be about resolving the problem.

3. **Make behaviors the issue, not personalities.** Don't do a character assassination. It will really tick a difficult man off and, in the long run, work against you (chapter 4).

4. **Don't make threats you're not willing to carry out.** In fact, don't make threats at all. If you want to take action, just do it.

5. **Don't adopt a superior attitude.** Feel superior inside, sound strong and in control of yourself outside (chapter 3).

6. **Don't stop listening.** In fact, do just the opposite. Really listen carefully. The difficult man will love it and spill more beans than he ever planned to.

TO ESCALATE OR NOT TO ESCALATE, THE CHOICE IS YOURS

How you initiate the discussion will either increase or decrease your difficult man's resistance to dealing with the situation. Here are some statements that escalate and some better alternatives that de-escalate.

Statements that escalate	Statements that de-escalate
"We need to talk, because we have a problem."	"I want to talk to you about...; it should take about 5 minutes." (Do not exceed 15 at first.)
"Don't you think that...?"	"Do you think that...?"
"Why did you...?	"Help me understand..." "What were your reasons for...?"
"I think we should..."	"This is what I want to do. What do you want to do?"

Often we use the phrases on the left side of the page with the best of intentions to open up a dialogue, and we are surprised when instead of making things better, we've made them worse. The only time to use the escalation phrases is when you have cut your emotional investment and are going for broke.

As women, we automatically escalate the conflict

and unintentionally set ourselves up as losers whenever we use backfiring words like "because." "Because" is the kind of word that triggers justifying, defending, and explaining. It gets us tangled up in our own position. Ninety-nine percent of the time, even though you don't owe difficult men an explanation, it's hard not to "because" someone. Your Destroyer Boss is demanding that you work overtime. "Sorry, I can't work overtime," you say, "because my child/husband/dog is expecting me." Now, your Destroyer threatens you with the idea that they'd go hungry if you had no job. So, replace this conflict-escalating statement with: "I'm not available to stay late this evening." Stop right before the "because" escapes your lips. Try to avoid overdefending your actions. If he demands an explanation, give it to him, courteously. Just don't spew, if it isn't necessary.

● CONFLICT-RESOLUTION ROUTES

So that you can deliberately choose the best way to go in tough situations with difficult men, I want to give you some routes to follow. This verbal road map may appear complex at first, but it's not. I'll take you through it one step at a time.

Route 1: DOING NOTHING.

This is like saying, "Leave well enough alone." You don't try to de-escalate or escalate the situation; in fact, you don't even let your difficult man know that there is a problem. When your difficult man is doing his difficult thing, instead of acknowledging it, you let it go. Not a bad strategy to use if there are people around, if you are so upset that you're afraid you will totally lose it if you even open your mouth, or if you have a low emotional investment in the issue. You are choosing to withdraw temporarily or permanently. So you say nothing, and your DM doesn't even know that he has said or done something you don't like.

Carol works as a hostess in a restaurant. One night, a man came in and asked for a table. Since he had no reservation and the restaurant was full, Carol told him that it would be about 40 minutes before he could be seated. In true Blamer fashion, the man chastised Carol, telling her in a loud and obnoxious voice that the wait was her fault because she wasn't doing her job properly. Carol looked at him, and all she said was, "Shall I put your name down on the waiting list?" Nothing more. She didn't change her tone of voice or take him on. There was no point, and since she was not the owner of the restaurant, she didn't have the power to bounce him out on his butt.

Route 2: GO FOR BROKE.

When you go for broke, you are engaging in battle with a might-makes-right approach. You are going for the win, hoping your difficult man will lose. It is an all-or-nothing move, and you can win big or lose big. You are forcing your position on the difficult man; with this choice, even if you win, beware. Your DM will probably try to get even, so although victory will be sweet, it will also be brief. If you know that you are absolutely unwilling to abide by what your difficult man wants, this may very well be your best choice.

Jill's boss wanted her to find some money in the budget for him to spend three extra nights in Las Vegas after his convention was over. He told her to doctor the books so that no one would know. She decided that she was unwilling to lie or do something dishonest for him, and she told him just that. She was ready for whatever consequences her assertiveness would bring; it was that important to her. (By the way, her boss got someone else to do it.)

Route 3: LET HIM HAVE HIS WAY.

This tactic means that you let your difficult man know that you disagree and want something different, and then go along with what he wants anyway. You give in. It is a smoothing action that I sometimes refer to as a banking method of conflict resolution. You are making a deposit now, by giving in, so that later you can (try to) make a withdrawal using guilt, a method we'll talk more about in the "Below the Belt" section, later in this chapter. Be careful though, sometimes the DM will not recognize that you've opened an account, and when you try to get a payback, he may not pay. As we discussed earlier, this is a good way to go when he has more of an emotional investment than you do.

June initially said no when Bob, her boss, asked her

to drop off some material at a client's office on her way home. The problem was, she was in a hurry, and the client's office wasn't on her way home at all. She was supposed to get home early, because her brother-in-law was coming to dinner, and her boss knew this. Upon thinking it through, however, she realized that going out of her way to do this for her boss would accomplish two things. First, her boss would look good to the client and as an Admiration Hound, that was important to him; and second, getting caught in traffic would mean an hour less that she'd have to spend with her obnoxious brother-in-law. She told her boss that she'd changed her mind and that she would take the time to do it.

Route 4: LET'S MAKE A DEAL.

This route requires that you split the difference. When you are willing to give your difficult man some of what he wants in order to get some of what you want, this is your move. It enables both of you to get at least a little bit, if not everything. It is a form of sharing. What's good about it is that if you are at an impasse, you can both agree to do the minimum and move on.

Ann had a plumber come to the house to fix a pipe that had broken. She asked for an estimate, and the plumber did a "there, there, little lady, don't worry about a thing" number on her, which she allowed. (Okay, she wasn't perfect, but she learned!) When he presented her with a megabill, she just about flipped. After much discussion (he said, "This is really cheap for what I had to do," and she, "I asked you to tell me how much it was before you started"), they split the difference. She still paid a little more than she wanted to, but she had no more water on the floor. The plumber left with enough money for what he had done. Not a great outcome, but satisfactory.

Route 5: WORK IT THROUGH.

This is the two-heads-are-better-than-one approach. You don't try to convince or push your DM to do it your way, and he doesn't try to convince or push you to do it his way. Together, you brainstorm and come up with a new solution to the problem that tickles both of you. It is wonderful when it happens, but don't hold your breath. Both of you have to be willing to put your cards on the table and show your hands. You have to be willing to put your egos aside, really listen and understand what the other is saying, and clearly define the problem and go through all the steps (chapter 4).

John wanted to meet with Trisha on Wednesday at 5:30. Trisha had an afternoon meeting and wanted to meet in the morning instead. At first, they went back and forth, but once they started discussing what each of them was dealing with regarding their schedules, they figured out that they could meet for lunch on Friday and it would work perfectly for both of them.

These routes can be used alone or in combination, depending upon what's needed to deal most effectively with your difficult man. You might choose to start by pretending it's not happening and then, when you're ready, move to putting it on the table and working it through. Use your own best judgement.

If you can, become familiar with all the conflict-resolution choices or routes. Don't just do what you've
always done without deciding if perhaps there is a better
choice, and if your selection is lousy, so be it. Have a
post-conflict discussion with yourself, your steering
wheel, or a trusted friend, and prepare to do better the
next time. Don't keep score; instead, keep trying. That's
what conflict savvy is all about.

● BELOW-THE-BELT TECHNIQUES

If you still aren't convinced that I am not above getting down and dirty, this section will probably do the
trick. Although I give the upcoming information to you
slightly tongue-in-cheek, it is, nonetheless, an important
part of your conflict-savvy repertoire. Timing is everything, or close to everything, and a big part of timing is
knowing when to pull out a totally different kind of
behavior. In this section, you will learn about three:
being helpless, pleading and groveling, and the creative
use of guilt, the gift that keeps on giving. I could add a
fourth, flattery, but it is so obvious that I will just remind
you now not to be above pulling it out when you need it.
The decision to use any or all of the three is a very personal one. There will be times when you have to decide
which is more important to you, being forthright or getting what you want.

BEING HELPLESS ◀

There may be times when the Testosterone Club is meeting and they just will not let you in. At such times, you could revert back to stereotypically female ways of operating. (You wouldn't have to tell anybody.)

Laura finds that many of the men in her business treat her like the "little lady." At first, their condescension bothered her; she would get upset and resist. But she found out that confronting them made things worse. Now when she deals with these difficult men, she really does act like the little lady and happily reports that she gets more than she ever hoped possible.

Such behavior isn't quite pleading and groveling, but it really isn't assertive, either! Again, I'm not telling you to imitate it, and I'm also not telling you not to. What does your radar pick up? Will the end justify the means? What is your emotional investment? Ultimately, you have to do what is right for you. Don't ever forget that.

PLEADING AND GROVELING ◀

As I said earlier, we can't talk about strategies for dealing with difficult men without giving pleading and groveling honorable mention at the very least. These strategies for what-to-do-when are rarely discussed in anything currently written about how women are supposed to deal with difficult men. As a very assertive woman, I do not normally use or recommend these skills, but they do have their place.

Kate wanted her boss, Larry, to give her a travel assignment to Europe. Larry was best buddies with Ralph, who also wanted to go. Kate knew that there was no reason why Larry had to give her the assignment, so when she began to feel Europe slipping through her fingers, she resorted to pleading and whining. She was relentless. Kate got the trip and made sure to drink a toast to Larry while sitting in a café near the Eiffel Tower. To her, it was worth it.

Not every DM situation is going to end with your getting everything you want; the law of averages is against you. Even though you may do the right thing at the right time in the right way, if your DM has a heavy investment in acting like the back end of a donkey—or in being "right," as he might put it—he just may not respond to anything you try. If this happens (and we hope that it doesn't), you then have to decide how far you are willing to go to come out on top.

You get the idea. Appearing to act out of weakness will often get you what you want, but you have to:

A. Really want what's on the table.

B. Do it for the sake of keeping your pleading and groveling skills primed and ready.

C. Want to see how far you can go with this technique.

D. Be pretty bored with the relationship.

The choice is yours.

WHAT'S WRONG WITH GUILT?
IT WORKS ◀

If you want to send a difficult man on a trip, it's fun every once in a while to make it a guilt trip. When we talked about conflict-resolution routes, we didn't discuss this one. Guilt has some connection to route 3, the letting-the-difficult-man-have-his-way option. It just takes it one step further and one step lower. Here's how it's done: you introduce the notion that you are going to give in and go along with what your difficult man wants; then, you start laying it on thick. You make sure that your difficult man has a full—and I do mean full—understanding of everything you are giving up for him, the sacrifices you are making, the loss and inconvenience that you feel, and then, to add that certain je ne sais quoi, the fact that your life or situation will be totally ruined, you're prepared for it.

Sending difficult men on guilt trips means helping them pack and making sure that they never forget how they got to where they are. When done well, making a difficult man feel guilty can be a thing of beauty, enough to bring a tear to the eye. When done poorly, it can backfire, so be careful. Don't hesitate to use helpless facial expressions, the kind we rejected as not making you look assertive in the body-language section in chapter 4. In this case, you really don't want to look assertive. It's a delicate balance we're going for here, not too strong but not a total victim either. Make sure that your tone of voice doesn't sound sarcastic. Pay attention to how you end your sentences, and don't point at your difficult man with your trigger finger. It will cloud your guilt message.

Brenda wanted Jack to go out of town with her to a trade show, which was happening right in the middle of the World Series. Jack was an avid baseball fan and had tickets to attend all of the games with his longtime baseball buddies. Brenda reminded Jack about the free week in Maui that she had sacrificed for him, as well as the expensive watch she had given him for his birthday (because he had said he wanted one), a purchase that had taken most of her savings. She then told him to "never mind," she would get one of the guys she worked with to escort her because his games were more important than their relationship, anyway; then, she sighed one of those lingering sighs. Jack went to the trade show.

You have probably used guilt quite successfully yourself many times in the past. It is a good technique to have in your pocket, as long as you don't overuse it. Like pleading and groveling, it fills a niche. It is one more way to deal with your difficult men, and I, for one, think that variety is the spice of life.

All of the ideas in this chapter work well, and the more adept you become at using them, the less of a chance your difficult man will have. Which brings us to an important and probably inevitable problem: backlash. Your difficult man just may not stand up and cheer when presented with the more in-control and less vulnerable you; in fact, he may—how shall we say this—act out? So read on to prepare yourself to jump this one last hurdle.

CHAPTER

6

How to Cope with
Negative Reactions

If you're a woman who has always been in the background and rarely speaks up, never questions, and always complies, you can be sure that difficult men will have different reactions to your change of behavior. Some may say, "Hey, that doesn't sound like you. Are you having a bad day?" Others may continue to try to dismiss your opinions because you are not known as the type of woman who seriously speaks up for what you want. They'll think that if they ignore you, your bad mood will blow over; and they'll get pretty nasty when they discover that it isn't a mood after all!

When you change your behavior, difficult men will have to change theirs. Many will find this inconvenient, more than likely resent it, and give you static about it. To help you understand that you have to look at the entire process rather than the immediate outcome, let's say you've always driven a car with an automatic transmission, and now, for the first time, you are learning to drive a car with a stick shift. At first, it's going to be a bumpy ride as the car responds differently to you, but eventually you are going to learn how to drive your new car smoothly and automatically. People may not want to be in the same car with you at first, but in time, they will get used to the idea while you get better at shifting.

Learning to speak your own mind instead of theirs follows the same process. When you begin to shift your behaviors, difficult men are going to respond differently to you, and you have to expect that their reaction may not always be positive. The first time you say, "I'm not available to do that" and then don't feel obliged to give a reason, they may say, "What's the matter with you?" Using what you have learned in this book and speaking up come with some risk, but the results are well worth it, even though the reactions may be sweat inducing. You need to be ready when the backlash comes.

Backlash usually involves put-downs and testing on the part of difficult men who, as we have already said, are not necessarily thrilled with your new approach to them. In this chapter we're going to take two different approaches to dealing with what they dish out: slice and dice, and charm. Once again, depending upon the difficult man, the situation, and your investment in it, you can choose which one will work best for you. Instead of separating them out, we'll look at degrees of both. We'll begin with some different ways to say no, then we'll move to the pocket guide to responding to put-downs. From here, we'll go to dealing with testing, and finally, how to deal for what you want.

● IT'S OKAY TO SAY NO

As a newly emerging in-control-of-yourself, speaking-your-mind type of woman, you will find yourself subjected to several unattractive verbal comments delivered by the pretty ticked off, not to mention confused, difficult men we've been discussing. Threatened or inconvenienced men pull no punches, as we'll see in their responses in the put-downs section. They do whatever it takes to hang on to what they want. They say whatever they can think of to get their point across. Let's say that you tell a difficult man, "I am not going to cook dinner tonight. I have more important things I need to do." Here are some of the destructive comments he might resort to:

1. **The threat:** "Let me put it this way: if you don't cook dinner for me, I'm not going to your family reunion next weekend."

2. **The put-down:** "Do you really think that any other man would put up with someone as spoiled as you?"

3. **The put-off:** "I have no time for this BS now; the game is starting."

4. **The denial:** "You're not too busy to cook dinner. You just don't manage your time well."

5. **The cold shoulder:** "Quit whining. I know dozens of women who would trade places with you in a minute."

6. **The order:** "Just get off your behind and do it!"

This is just a sampling of what you might have to deal with. I offered it to get you in the mood for a technique I want you to learn by heart, the technique of saying no.

It is okay to say no. You don't have to feel guilty about it. Nowhere is it written that yes is the only acceptable answer you can give a difficult man. You have to be willing and able to set limits, even if it feels awkward at first.

Here's an example: You refuse to go to your significant other's class reunion. You're retaining water, feel like a blob, and don't want to see (or be seen by) the other guys that you dated from his class before you got married. Your S.O. reacts by getting angry and makes the same demand again.

How do you respond?

A. I'm confused. I thought we had resolved this, and I would hate to have it surface again and destroy our relationship.

B. What you're doing right now, bringing this issue up again, is making things worse.

C. I've made my decision.

Don't underestimate the impact of each of the above three choices; they are all very strong. Even though they are charming, they still say no.

Such a simple little word. Two regular little letters, but what power they have when they come together. Sometimes they have so much power that you have to soften them a little. The way to do it depends upon how you want to come across.

If you want to be:	Make NO sound like this:
Strong	No. I am unwilling to do it.
Understanding	I can see that this is a problem for you, and I can understand what you're going through.
Charming	I really appreciate the opportunity you're offering me. Thank you. No.
Noncommittal	It sounds really great. Maybe next time.
Very definite	Definitely not.
Enthusiastic	I love that idea. Since I can't do it, I know that when you ask them, someone else will just jump at the chance.

If you want to be:	Make NO sound like this:
Disappointed.............	I wish you had asked me yesterday, before I made another commitment.
Humble	I'm flattered that you'd choose me. It won't work out, but I appreciate your asking.

Practice makes perfect. Try these to get the hang of them. It's fun to watch the reactions difficult men have. You'll see confusion, surprise, horror, and who knows what else. Enjoy it! As a side note, I also find these great to use when I get telephone solicitations at home at night, when I least appreciate them.

● THE POCKET GUIDE TO RESPONDING TO PUT-DOWNS

Now that you have gotten your feet wet in the no department, let's go a step further. There's a difference between saying no and responding to put-downs, which is what you'll get once you start saying no. When difficult men realize what's happening, they may say some nasty things. These can be insulting and demeaning, and I have seen women let themselves be destroyed by them.

You can survive them and actually use them to your advantage.

Answering put-downs is better done in private, but sometimes you might need to do so in public. When this happens, a little humor can be really helpful in buffering the sting. The following put-downs are presented with a range of possible responses, some funny, some serious, and some with a tinge of sarcasm. The smaller your emotional investment is, the more likely you will be to use sarcasm. Look at each situation and relationship individually, consult your head, consult your gut, and proceed.

In addition, the following responses use either the charm or the slice-and-dice approach. As you read them, see if you can find some that you would feel comfortable using. You can think up more of your own. Remember that your tone of voice and body language can make any message sound either charming or slicing and dicing and that slicing and dicing is very confrontational.

When he says:	You respond:
You're too sensitive.	I like that about myself. It makes me feel human.
	Funny, it works for me.
	Soft on the outside, crying on the inside, that's me. I like the fact that I'm consistent.

When he says:	You respond:
You're too emotional.	I am not a programmed robot, and as a person with feelings, I will react. I am emotional because I have deep feelings about this.
	My being emotional has nothing to do with it.
	What would be different if I were less emotional?
	I am emotional because I care. Do you care?
	Alert the media. You recognized a feeling!
Lighten up.	If I'm heavy, it's because I care a lot about this.
	This *is* lighter; you should have seen me yesterday.
	I'm light enough for me.
I didn't mean anything by it.	Does that mean you'll never do it again?
	Does it matter to you that I didn't like it?
	What could you replace it with?

When he says:	You respond:
I hug everybody.	Am I the first person who has asked you not to?
	It's hard for me to tell you this, yet it is so important that I will. I feel uncomfortable when you hug me.
	Except me, from now on.
If I didn't like you, I wouldn't say it.	That's not how it sounds to me.
	Somehow, this doesn't make me feel better.
	What *would* you say if you didn't like me?
If you loved me, you'd lose weight and want to look nice for me.	I wish it were that easy.
	Weight is more important to you than it is to me.
	My weight has nothing to do with my love for you.
	You're right. If I loved you, I would.
Don't you think you should?	Do you think I should? Oh, we disagree.
	No, I don't.

When he says:	You respond:
Don't be so serious.	My being serious means I respect what you're saying.
	When I listen well, I get serious.
	My "serious control knob" is broken.
If I were you, I'd...	I always enjoy hearing about the differences between us.
	That does sound like something you would do.
	I guess it's lucky you're not me.
You're the only one who...	It isn't important to me to fit in.
	I like feeling special and unique.
	Once again, I'm a trailblazer. Is that a problem for you?
Why are you making a big deal about this?	I'm willing to spend time and energy on something that is important to me.
	What would you prefer I do?
	Why are you?

When he says:	**You respond:**
I haven't got time to talk about it now.	Are you willing to make the time since it is very important to me?
	When will you have time? Tonight or tomorrow morning?
	You don't have time to not talk about it.
Have you gained a little weight?	Is my weight of interest to you?
	Compared to what?
	Let's talk about you instead of me.
That was a dumb thing to say.	If you were saying it, what would have been different?
	Is it different from what you wanted me to say?
	I'll try to say it differently.
Boy! That was stupid.	Does "stupid" mean that you disagree?
	What were you hoping for?
	Define "stupid."

When he says:	You respond:
I can't believe you said that.	What specifically are you referring to?
	Is there something in particular that you are having trouble with?
	Believe it. I said that.
I can't believe you would do that.	Is it different from what you wanted me to do?
	What can I do to clarify what I did?
	Believe it. I would.
Do you know how many women would kill to be in your position?	Are you asking whether or not I appreciate you?
	They're desperate. I'm above that.
You're not happy unless you're making my life miserable.	Making your life miserable is not my intent.
	What, specifically, are you referring to?
	I'm sorry you feel that way.
	True. How am I doing?

When he says:	You respond:
What makes you so special?	Do you really think I'm special or are you being sarcastic?
	A lot of things.
	How much time do you have?
Having PMS? Don't tell me, you're a charter member of the PMS Strike Force!	What's your point?
	It depends on what you **are** asking me to do.
	Are you?
	I hear a little hostility there. Tell me, what is concerning you?
	If you mean am I strong-willed and not always easy to get along with, yes.
	Yes, I am.
(He says nothing but rolls his eyes)	You just rolled your eyes. What does that mean?
	If you had spoken instead of rolling your eyes, what would you have said?
	Do you have something in your eye?

When he says:	You respond:
What happened to the sweet little girl I married?	She grew up.

As you read through these, I hope you were able to see a pattern. Most of the more caustic comments, though definite conflict escalators, are good for one-shot deals from which you can afford to walk away. The relationship-building responses, on the other hand, were geared toward either giving the difficult man specific information or engaging the difficult man to give you more information. This is just one more way to use the questions we learned about in "Getting the Information You Want Without Getting Their Goat" in chapter 4; and the more you use questions that are probing, the more information you'll have to work with to defuse the difficult man's hostility.

● HOW TO DEAL WITH TESTING

Aside from biting comments, what other kinds of behavior can you expect from a difficult man struggling to hold on to what he has? It depends a lot on his reaction to your new approach to dealing with him. If he feels threatened, he may lash out and become (more) obnoxious, or he may withdraw and use more passive or passive-aggressive behaviors. An Innie may become more verbal, and an Outie might become more so or much more low-key. In any event, one thing is inevitable: there will be a testing phase. Testing is merely an extension of the denial your difficult man will experience because he doesn't want to accept the fact that you can't go home again. By that, I mean what we talked about in chapter 3: the party is over, the rules have changed, and you've removed 911 from your forehead.

Some difficult men may actually worry about their virility as a result of your becoming stronger. When you threaten this part of the difficult male's ego, his reaction might be interesting, to say the least, and he may feel compelled to test you to see how he stacks up against the new you. He may test you to see just how far he can go and how much he can still influence you. He may feel compelled to check your Testosterone Deference Quotient.

Difficult men are very transparent. It is easy to see if their issue is control, acceptance, intellectual dominance, emotional security, egocentricity, or anything else. The way they test you will tell you this.

Listen to the conversation Gretchen had with her (now ex-) husband years ago when she started traveling as part of her job, and he wanted to see whether he was still the king of the castle.

> He: *"You can't go. You have all these responsi-bilities: the house, the yard, dinner..."*

> She: *"Wait a minute. If you told me that you had to go, what would I say to you?"*

> *He:* "You'd probably say, 'Where are you going, how long will you be gone, and is there anything I need to pack or do for you?'"
>
> *She:* "So why is this different? What should you be saying to me? Since we are both working for a living, we both have obligations we have to keep."

Gretchen didn't attack him for trying to see how far he could go to get her to change. She used probing questions to bring the situation into focus.

Gloria deals with testing at the office. When the issue of sexist language comes up, everyone looks to her, because she is responsible for cleaning it up and getting the men to change their vocabulary. "Traditional terms like 'man hours' or 'we have to man the booth' are something that the men I supervise don't want to give up. When they use such terminology, I always smile first and then say, 'staff hours' and 'staff the booth.' And they say, 'Come on, no one minds "man" in these situations.' To which I answer, 'Would you like to start calling it "woman hours" and "woman the booth"?' When they laugh and say, 'We wouldn't mind,' I laugh and tell them, 'So do it.' And then they say, 'staff hours' and 'staff the booth.'"

As women, we have to understand that it's difficult for men to change their habits, and that they will keep testing to see how many they can keep. Gloria often tries to use humor. "Sometimes they groan and roll their eyes and I just smile my best and cutest feminine smile, and they groan once more and give in. At my level, the put-downs I get are generally done with humor. Difficult men wouldn't dare to take me on face-to-face without a lot of humor, so I'm able to respond in kind. The messages are clear."

Humor is an important part of the charming approach. It can lighten up a potentially heavy and uncomfortable situation. Many women have found that in any male-dominated situation at work, they have to start by proving themselves and their ability to do the job and take what men dish out. Having done that, then they are able to joke and be charming. The reason? Men recognize women as people, rather than as just women doing a previously male-defined job. It is a given: working in a male environment, women will be tested on their qualifications and their personalities. Once men know women can do it, and take it, they stop challenging and start relating.

Gloria has gone through more "difficult-men torture testing cases" than most of the women I know put together, but I particularly like this situation:

There was a guy where she worked known to swear like a sailor and have no respect for anybody or anything except his own boss. As a result, when he disagreed with anyone else's decisions, he would yell and curse at them. One day, he did this to Gloria. She picked up the telephone, and heard a booming voice say, "I just heard your decision on... What the hell is wrong with you? Do you have shit for brains? There's no way in hell that I am going to let shit like this happen!"

At which point, she thought to herself, "Who is this person? I'm not going to take this abuse." So she said, "If you think you can call and curse at me over the telephone, you're wrong. I'll hang up. If you've got a problem, tell me what it is and I'll listen. Then, I'll discuss it with you. Never call and curse at me again." And he never did. He pushed as hard as he could to see where he could go, and he got his answer. Nowhere.

Flight attendants who work in first class, where it seems as though difficult men are almost the only type admitted, are experts on being charming and dealing with testing. Granted they don't always deal with backlash, but they do get the brunt of whatever the difficult man has been up against all day. And they are in stereotypically sexist roles, which means that men expect them to back down.

Connie's approach is simple: "I treat them as if they are little boys in grown-up bodies. That way, I know just what to expect, which is not much, and how to deal with them, which is easy. I treat them like children—with respect, but like immature people who haven't been socialized to know how to behave."

Carla takes it one step further: "Since I know I can outthink and outsmart them, I make a game out of seeing how long it takes to get them right where I want them, in the palm of my hand."

For a long time, Joanne worked on commuter flights heavily traveled by men who had been wheeling and dealing all day. As a result, they were often downright nasty by the time they boarded the plane. She explained her tactics this way: "Early on, I learned to pick out the men with the tight jaws and the most tense expressions, so that when they sprang into action and started making demands and yelling at me, I was ready with my most sympathetic 'I want to please you' manners. One of my best responses has always been 'I hope I can make your day better, as of right now.' I'm not in a power-play with these difficult men. I just want to make sure that they don't feel compelled to act out in order to prove themselves to me. I charm them into submission." Difficult men can be like big babies. When they lash back because they don't get their way, you really can deal with them. Watch for clues so that you can head them off; sometimes all it takes is a smile, at other times a little teasing. Charm and grace under pressure go a long way.

Merilee is a very successful former actress who is now active in business and interacts with very powerful men. "I never put them on the defensive. The most important lesson I've learned is to defend myself without attacking. I try to be polite and charming, with impeccable manners. I've learned to communicate my thoughts and feelings as clearly as I can. I've found that they may not come over to my way of thinking, but if I'm courteous, at least they'll listen, and that's half the battle. That's the way I have many more victories than defeats. My brand of charm often includes humor. I can say almost anything with a friendly laugh and get my point across. I don't go for the jugular. I don't have to prove anything."

How do men test a woman at work? They probe the outer limits of her knowledge and skill by asking her a lot of questions, posing problems, and pushing to find out how she would theoretically handle various situations. Then they watch to see how she copes with adversity, whether or not she becomes "too emotional," and how much of a good sport she is. They wait to see whether she blames others or is a team player. In many cases, women have been given jobs that they were not ready for, have fallen apart doing them, and then have been banished from other key positions because they "weren't cut out to be in the trenches."

If you are not impetuous, if you are in control, if you are not mean, and if you can laugh at yourself, you will get through the testing phase and graduate to being accepted.

In dealing with backlash, what complicates matters is that slice-and-dice and charm are just a voice inflection, facial expression, or hand gesture away from each other. To do either well, you have to pay attention to the skills we learned in chapter 4, and the conflict guidelines we reviewed in chapter 5.

You have to be prepared to deal with put-downs by either ignoring or responding to them. You have to be willing to say no in whatever manner feels right to you at the time; you have to be ready to deal with and endure the testing that will eventually occur; and you will do yourself a favor if you anticipate ways in which you can strike deals for the behavior you want from difficult men.

The toughest change you will have to make as you deal with backlash is overcoming the tendency to back down—to say that you didn't mean anything by what you said or did and to decide that it's not worth it and that you'll just do what you've always done. Backlash can be very draining; it can wear you down, but do whatever you have to in order to stand firm. Pop some extra vitamins. Get a telephone support buddy. Whatever works for you. There is too much at stake for you to risk caving in. No matter how many times your difficult man asks you to cover and take the blame for him in a meeting or not say anything when his brother grabs your behind at the Sunday dinner, don't give in. Practice in advance.

There is a funny definition of insanity I've heard that is relevant here. Insanity is "doing the same thing over and over again, but expecting the results to be different." Difficult men will keep on testing and hoping that even after you have begun to use your new skills, you will change your behavior back to what it was. Give it up, guys!

Or as Brenda says, "Face it; all difficult men are like frogs," and to this I once again add, this doesn't mean that women have to be lily pads.

7

Get Used to
Success

It is not always easy adjusting to relationships with used-to-be-difficult men. You may feel pressured to take more responsibility for keeping your relationships open and honest. You no longer have an excuse for acting like a victim. As in a tug of war, when the difficult men stop tugging, you have to stop as well or you'll fall flat on your face.

You need to be prepared to give up your anger and replace it with a sense of enjoyment and accomplishment. Can you let go of the pain and the resentment? Here are a few last-minute adjustments to help you do so.

TESTOSTERONE DEFERENCE SYNDROME RECOVERY— ONE DAY AT A TIME

Throughout this book we have been talking about the various processes involved in dealing with difficult men. You and your difficult man started out in opposite corners, whether the differences were spoken out loud or not. You've begun to change your behavior and he's begun to change his. Can you stop reading now? Too soon. You have narrowed the gap, but you have not sealed it airtight. Change that happens overnight rarely sticks. People (men and women, difficult and otherwise) attend one of my one-day seminars and by the end of the day are chomping at the bit to change their worlds. Sometimes I almost have to block the door so they don't leave and head straight for a major letdown. Since you're wherever you are and I'm not in the same room with you, I can't block your exit, but I can stress the importance of proceeding slowly.

As a woman, you have probably unknowingly suffered from Testosterone Deference Syndrome for a long time. It has undoubtedly shaped your world to a great extent, and has influenced who you are, what you do, and whom you do it with. And now, even though you have adjusted your attitude, it will not behoove you to try to overhaul all your old beliefs and subsequent behaviors at once. Don't expect to go from a moth to a butterfly in microwave time. Don't look at every man as a potential assertiveness exercise; it would be too exhausting for you and for them. Don't turn into the consummate charming southern belle, either, or you will have difficult men everywhere, either laughing or throwing up on your shoes from all the sugar you're doling out.

As much as I dislike the word *moderation*, this really is a good time to bring it up. Just because you're reading the last chapter of this book doesn't mean you're finished. You do have an excellent chance of permanently changing the dynamics of your relationships with difficult men, but if you do it too fast, you will tick them off, confuse them thoroughly, or behave in a way that you may not be willing or able to sustain.

By now you have a lot of options available to you. You have learned several techniques and have had an opportunity to begin the process of adjusting your self-esteem (upward).

You now know that you will be able to overcome the Testosterone Deference Syndrome because you have changed the way you look at difficult men, yourself, and the situations you find yourself in. By the same token, you now hopefully feel much better about yourself. You have exchanged blame for planning and self-consciousness for curiosity. You have decided that you don't have to be as tough as nails or as soft as a marshmallow.

Take a few minutes now to reflect on the major beliefs you have rejected about TDS in the following areas: (1) what it entitled the bearer to say; (2) what it entitled the bearer to do; (3) what it meant about his intelligence in relation to yours.

If you really don't hold those old beliefs anymore, the next part of your recovery should be a real snap!

We each have our own methods of setting ourselves

up for failure in dealing with difficult men. Either we expect too much of ourselves or we expect too much of them. Again, to keep you going after the initial rush of your jump-start has subsided, it will be important for you to give yourself some positive affirmations, regardless of the ups and downs you are experiencing on a day-to-day basis. Here are some that I suggest. Read them and add a few of your own.

TDSR Affirmations List

1. I can cope with anything a difficult man throws my way.

2. I have a lot of good ideas that I can put into practice.

3. I have to expect that I will screw up some situations.

4. I have a lot of power and I can choose whether or not I want to use it.

5. I don't have to prove anything to anybody.

6. I deserve the best I can get. I am that important.

7. I create my own reality. The best way to get positive relationships is to create them myself.

Now, add some of your own:

8.

9.

10.

11.

12.

Put this list where you can see and get to it easily and read it every day—twice a day when you have a difficult man to deal with.

● HOW TO AVOID BACKSLIDING

When you begin taking better care of yourself and enjoying the fruits of your labor, you won't want to backslide. Your desire, however, may not be enough to keep you going forward, especially if you are dealing with sporadic backlash. In addition to using your affirmations, you'll need to have a plan, an agreement that you make with yourself to make sure you stay on track. In implementing your antibacksliding plan, ask yourself—and answer—these four questions:

1. What difficult-man behavior am I going to deal with?

2. What exactly am I going to do?

3. How am I going to do it?

4. What resistance should I prepare for?

If you don't shortcircuit backsliding and stop it before it starts, you might end up like a case of boiled frog. Sound disgusting? It is disgusting, and I'll tell you why. It is a well-known though slightly esoteric fact that if you put a live frog into a pot of boiling water, it immediately knows that it is not in a good place to be. (It probably flashes back to its tadpole days and flashes forward to its legs being sautéed in garlic butter.) As a result, it immediately tries to jump out of the water. If you put the very same frog into a pot of cool water and gradually turn up the heat to the boiling point, the frog will do nothing except go to sleep. I have a good reason for telling you this. Stay with me here. There is a logical connection. If you have a bla- tantly horrific experience with a difficult man, it will keep you on your toes and on the case, as it were. But if you have instances of little or no consequence, and you let them pass without ever evaluating your overall strategy, it won't be long until you're back in the same old rut or pot. So don't snooze in a pot of lukewarm water. Expect posi- tive experiences and you'll create them.

Backsliding conjures up an image of a woman sailing backward down a long metal chute, hopefully with some padding on her rear end so she doesn't bruise it when she lands, legs straight up and arms who-knows-where. If you don't want to put yourself in this picture, make sure that you don't make the 10 most common mistakes that lead to backsliding:

1. **Don't become too cocky** (pardon the pun). Difficult men are amazingly creative. Just because you've seen one routine doesn't mean you've seen them all.

2. **Don't be afraid to ask for help** from a friendly source. I always suggest starting DWDMSG (Dealing With Difficult Men Support Groups) or becoming a DM buddy with another woman.

3. **Don't discount all men as difficult.** They're not. A lot of men think that other men are just as obnoxious and ridiculous as you do. Some of the best insights I've gotten have been from men.

4. **Don't broadcast the new you to the world.** Many women make the mistake of boasting or bragging to anyone who'll listen. Resist the urge. Congratulate yourself quietly.

5. **Don't think that once is enough.** We talked about difficult men testing women to determine how much they can get away with and exactly what it would take to undermine their new attitude and behavior. Prepare yourself for repetition.

6. **Don't get so caught up that you carry the banner for all women.** You are not all women; you'll burn yourself out if you take the Robyn Hood approach.

7. **Don't expect to be liked and heralded by other women for taking control of yourself with difficult men.** Some of them may feel threatened, and others, still suffering from Testosterone Deference Syndrome, may resent you even disagreeing with a man.

8. **Don't forget to acknowledge the progress you make, even if it isn't monumental.** Just put one foot in front of the other and appreciate that you are moving forward.

9. **Don't stop trusting yourself.** If you take action that doesn't quite work out as you had hoped, don't begin to doubt your gut or your intellect. Difficult men are not machines, and, darn it, they don't always do what we expect.

10. **Don't worry; start working.** Decide to continually upgrade your how-and-what-to-do-when skills. There is always something new to learn.

Taking responsibility for improving the situations with the difficult men in your life can be very exciting. If you have a plan and you execute that plan, you get to do one of two things: enjoy your success or plan for the next time with a lot more experience under your belt. I said it earlier, and I'll say it again; it is up to you to bring these ideas to life, to allow them to work for you as you get stronger and more competent. Take the time and make it happen.

Another method that you might find useful is to have a two-way conversation with yourself. We joke a lot about people who talk to themselves, but I, for one, think it's a great idea. It is the ultimate control experience. You get to ask the questions and give the answers. If you feel yourself backsliding or backing away from the plate instead of stepping up to it, ask yourself (and then answer) these questions:

1. What exactly am I trying to accomplish?

2. What makes it important to deal with it at this particular time?

3. What is my plan?

4. What will it look like in action?

5. What will I get from using it?

6. What are my concerns?

7. What reactions might I get?

8. Have I planned well for resistance or backfires?

9. Is it worth the risk?

10. How will I feel after I've done it?

After you've answered these questions, put them aside for a little while and then go back to them. Give yourself some time to become slightly more objective when you read what you've written. Make any changes you think valid or necessary and give yourself a pat on the back for keeping the momentum going in the right direction.

● ENJOYING NEW RELATIONSHIPS WITH USED-TO-BE-DIFFICULT MEN

Try to recall when you first bought or received this book. At that time, when you thought about dealing with the most difficult men in your life, how would you have rated yourself on this Dealing With Difficult Men Anxiety Scale?

0	1	2	3	4	5
cool as a cucumber	very slight anxiety	mild anxiety	moderate anxiety, getting nervous	pretty nervous, beginning to panic	over the edge

And now, rate yourself after reading this book:

0	1	2	3	4	5

Each stage of this scale is typical of what women go through during their approach to dealing with difficult men. It's amazing what a little knowledge and confidence can do. With practice, you can make sure that you remain at the lower end of the scale. In fact, you are probably pretty close to erasing numbers 3, 4, and 5 already. Number 2 will go after you've had a few more positive experiences. There is no mystery to it. Practice makes as close to perfect as you can get. You will in fact find that in your dealings with difficult men, you will trade insecurity for respect, and in many cases, it will be mutual. Both of you will become more secure, and both of you will respect yourselves and each other a lot more. Carla told her husband, "If you will step back and give me a chance to be who I want to be, I think that you'd like me a lot more." He did, and he does. Sure, sometimes you will be lucky to arrive at minimal tolerance, because there are always a few holdouts, but don't underestimate your newfound power.

I have a big emotional investment in you and your success right now. You and I have gone through a lot together as you've read this book. I have shared a lot of my own experiences with you. You've listened to me whine, laugh, and poke fun at a lot of the difficult men who have passed through and continue to pass through my life and the lives of the women I have known. I have tried to make it as easy for you as possible, to make it okay for you to feel your feelings and do something constructive with them. I have tried to get you ready to enjoy your new relationships with used-to-be-difficult men. Sure, some might be still, and others might be again, but it really doesn't matter. You can handle it. You know how to be tough, you know how to be factual, you know how to be charming, and you know how to play with them. Face it, you know this stuff. You're graduating.

The world of difficult men is your oyster. Congratulate yourself on all you've accomplished. Be good to yourself when you fall on your face. Laugh at yourself as you pick yourself up. Appreciate yourself for not giving up.

The next time a difficult man tries to take you on or put you down, before you even open your mouth, think of me in the background. I'll be laughing up a storm, knowing what he has in store for him.